MACA

MACAU

Shann Davies
Photography by Richard Dobson

Hong Kong

Copyright © 1993 The Guidebook Company Ltd, Hong Kong

All rights reserved

Distribution in the United Kingdom, Ireland, Europe and certain Commonwealth countries by Hodder & Stoughton, Mill Road, Dunton Green, Sevenoaks, Kent TW13 2YA

British Library Cataloguing-in-Publication Data
A catalogue record for this book is available from the British Library

Grateful acknowledgement is made to the following authors and publishers for permissions granted:

Glidrose Publications for
Thrilling Cities by Ian Fleming © Glidrose Productions Ltd. 1963

Random House Inc and Faber and Faber Limited for
W H Auden: Collected Poems by W H Auden edited by Edward Mendelson © 1945, renewed 1973 by W H Auden

Oxford University Press for
City of Broken Promises by Austin Coates © Austin Coates

Editor: Don J Cohn
Illustrations Editor: Caroline Robertson
Map Design: Bai Yiliang

Photography by Richard Dobson
Additional photography courtesy of Macau Government Tourist Office 20 (lower left), 21, 40–41, 56 (above); Wattis Fine Art 49, 52

Production House: Twin Age Limited, Hong Kong
Printed in Hong Kong by Sing Cheong Printing Co Ltd

Macau post box

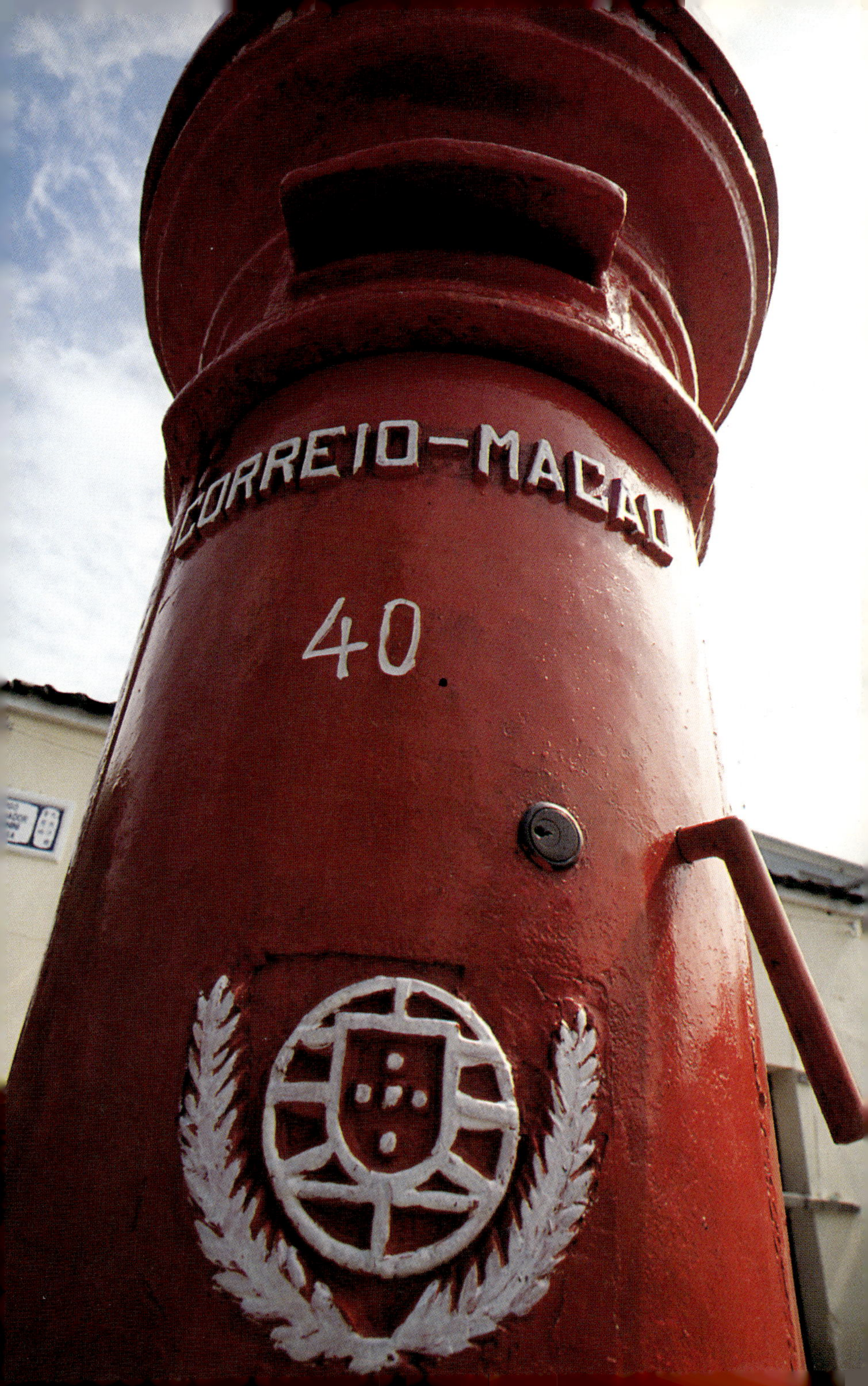
CORREIO-MACAU
40

Contents

EUROPE'S FIRST OUTPOST IN CHINA	10
FACTS FOR THE TRAVELLER	17
Getting There	17
Visas	18
Customs	18
Currency	19
Language	19
Communications	19
Climate and Clothing	19
Public Holidays	22
Getting Around and Touring	23
Entertainment	25
Sport	30
Cross-Cultural Cuisine	34
Shopping	35
Festivals of East and West	39
MUSEUMS, ART GALLERIES AND ARCHIVES	45
SIGHTS	51
Chinese Ancestry—Temples and Shrines	51
Imperial Imperative—Fortresses Then and Now	61
City of the Name of God—Churches & Charities	75
The Colonial Presence—Stately Homes and Offices	86
Chinese Shop-houses, Macanese Terraces	96
Modern Macau	102
Gardens and Grottoes	103
Cemeteries	106
RECOMMENDED READING	110
PRACTICAL INFORMATION	118
Hotels and Guesthouses	118
Restaurants	126
Useful Addresses	134
CHRONOLOGY	138
EXCURSIONS TO ZHONGSHAN AND ZHUHAI	143
Getting There	145
Visas	146
Tours and Touring	147
Sports and Entertainment	150
Practical Information	151
INDEX OF PLACES	156
SPECIAL TOPICS	
Don't Call it a Colony	15
The Battle of 1622	64

Explorers and Adventurers	70
Suggested Tour Itineraries	98
'There is None More Loyal'	108
Seaplane Sagas	141
Tower-house Villages	144
Dr Sun Yat-sen	146

EXCERPTS

Ian Fleming *on The Central Hotel*	24
Peter Mundy *on early impressions of Macau*	48
Manuel Barbosa *on the Portuguese Influence*	74
Austin Coates *on Macau houses*	88
W H Auden *on the growth of Macau*	154
Lin Tse-hau *on a visit to Macau*	155

MAPS

Macau	12
Early Map of Macau	49
Macau Centre	69
Taipa and Coloane Islands	84
Zhuhai and Surrounding Area	142

Europe's First Outpost in China

So now her flag to every gale unfurled
She towers the Empress of the Eastern world,
Such are the blessings sapient Kings bestow,
And from thy stream such gifts, O Commerce, flow.

In the *Os Lusiados*, Portugal's national poet Camões paid tribute to his country's explorers and merchant adventurers with classical European hyperbole but much truth. Thanks to the genius of Price Henry the Navigator—who believed Marco Polo's incredible tales and set out to rediscover fabulous Cathay—Portugal became a global trader, responsible for changing the commercial patterns of Europe and China. The capital of Portugal's eastern empire was Goa, but its keystone was Macau, a tiny settlement on the southwest lip of the Pearl River estuary, 145 kilometres (90 miles) south of Canton (Guangzhou), China's traditional centre for international trade.

The Portuguese founded Macau in 1557 with the blessing of local Chinese authorities (who they called 'mandarins' from *mandar*, to command) although no formal treaty was signed. By that time the Ming emperors had lost interest in the outside world, which they declared had nothing to offer the Celestial Kingdom. Trade was restricted to necessities and excluded dealings with Japan, whose pirates terrorized the coast. The Japanese rulers, attempting to escape China's awesome shadow, also banned trade between the two.

However, there were merchants in the southern parts of both countries eager to barter Japanese silver for Chinese silks. The Portuguese, with their fast, well-armed fleet of caravels, were the ideal entrepreneurs and Macau an ideal gateway to China and entrepôt for trade between Asia, Europe and the Portuguese empire.

Within 20 years, Macau had become an international city and one of the richest places on earth, thanks to investment in the cargoes shipped through the port. The Portuguese fleet would arrive from Goa via Malacca with the winds of the mid-summer monsoon. In their holds were luxuries from around the world: clocks and telescopes from Europe, ivory and live animals from Africa, damascenes and falcons from Arabia, muslin and precious gems from India, birds' nests and shark fins from Siam, spices and sandalwood from the East Indies, fruits and feathers from Brazil.

Most of this bounty was bartered at Canton for silks, which were shipped the next season to the Japanese port of Nagasaki and sold locally for silver. Returning to Macau in the spring, the 200 or so merchants who sailed with each voyage went back to Canton to buy silk, porcelain and assorted chinoiserie which they would sell in Europe—along with spices and exotic foodstuffs.

(Preceding pages) *Microlighting over Macau's Inner Harbour*

The effect of this trade on all parties was profound. In the last quarter of the 16th century, it drained fully one half of Japan's silver reserves. At the same time, although the Mandarins didn't realize it, the barbarian West had arrived to stay. Meanwhile, European commerce had shifted irrevocably from Venice and the Mediterranean to the Atlantic. Portuguese cargoes were now brokered by merchants in Antwerp, Amsterdam and later London. And when the Asian cargoes proved too costly for the traditional merchant houses, they had to band together to finance them, and capitalism was born.

Equally significant were the changes in European life, with silk transforming the way people dressed, spices revolutionizing the way they ate, oriental art inspiring painters and writers, and oriental ideas challenging established philosophy.

Western ideas were also filtering into Japan and China via Macau's Jesuit College. The Nuncio for the East, Francis Xavier, had died waiting to enter China in 1552, but his work in Japan was carried on by scholar-priests like Alessandro Valignano, Gaspar Vilela (who secured Nagasaki for the Jesuits) and João Rodrigues, the brilliant linguist who features in the book (and film) Shōgun.

The Jesuits assigned to China were an even more impressive lot. Best known are Matteo Ricci, Adam Schall von Bell and Ferdinand Verbiest, who went on to become honoured residents of the Peking court, where they taught Western science, cannon-casting and the Word of God. They all studied in the college that adjoined St Paul's, learning the languages and customs of Asia, while Christian converts from Japan and China worked alongside them, studying Western beliefs, art and sciences.

For Macau it was too good to last and the golden age came to an abrupt end when the Japanese closed up international shop in 1639 (except for a token Dutch presence), and two years later the Dutch took command of the vital sea-lanes to India with the capture of Malacca. By now, the rest of Europe had wind of the Portuguese discovery that China was Marco Polo's Cathay. The Portuguese celebrated their independence from Spain in 1640 (after 60 years of Spanish dynasty) but the explorations had beggared the country of money and men. Now it was the turn of new mercantile powers like Holland and Britain. They had the necessary funds, better and fresh fleets and the determination to take a share of the China trade. Iberians invoked 'discovery rights', but now the new European powers invoked 'conqueror rights' to enter oriental seas and emporiums.

By 1622 the Dutch had failed in their attempt to capture Macau. They had also tried to force the Chinese to grant them their own settlement, but soon discovered that the mandarins preferred to deal exclusively with the Western barbarians they knew—the Portuguese in Macau. As a result, from the late 17th century to the 1830s, merchants from Europe and the Americas set up trading offices in the Portuguese city and employed its residents as clerks, caretakers and concubines.

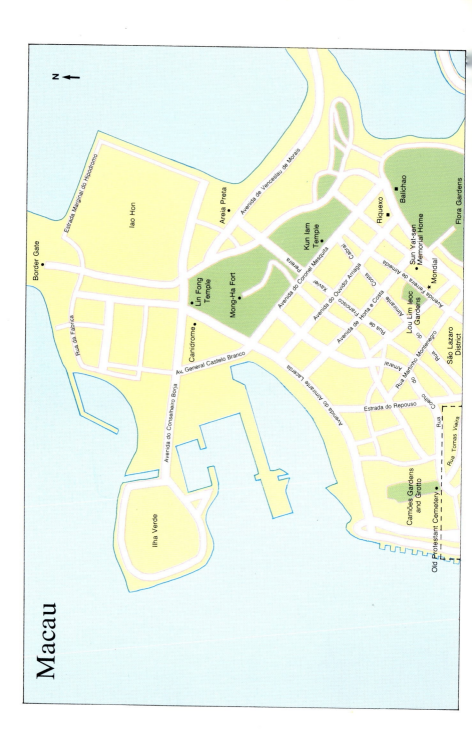

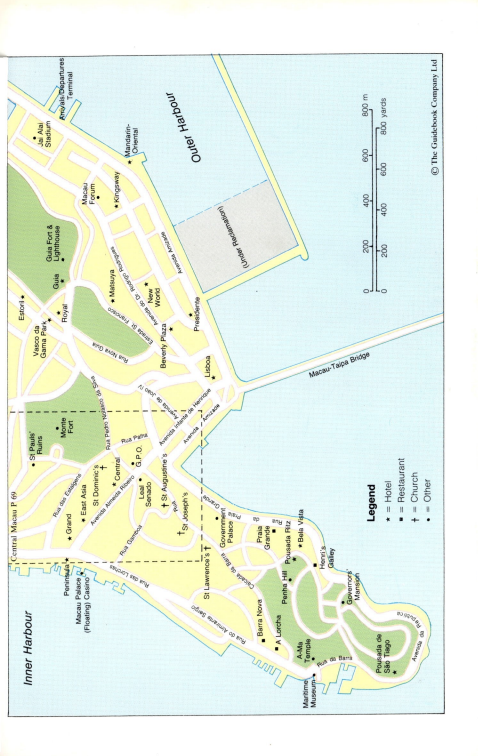

Macau accepted its fate and survived on the rentals of foreign merchants to supplement the reduced revenues from its own trade with China. The city continued to be a major port for merchants, missionaries, adventurers and ambassadors, who were invariably treated with hospitality. Contemporary descriptions dwell on the poverty and dissolution as well as the handsome new churches.

In the late 18th century, the city became a summer retreat for foreign merchants who spent the winter season in Canton. Increasingly, trade meant opium and tea: the 'drug' being the only commodity that could pay for Britain's ever-growing demand for the drink. The Chinese tried to reassert their Celestial Kingdom mandate, only to be defeated by the British in the Opium Wars.

Macau shared in the defeat when, as part of the peace treaty, Hong Kong was ceded to the British in 1841. Most of the foreign merchants moved to the new colony with its superior harbour, and the Portuguese territory, desperate for revenue, abolished all customs duties and legalised gambling. The latter move helped to save the city by attracting Hong Kong residents to the casinos—and drawing prudish condemnation from the opium-merchant civic leaders of Hong Kong.

As if to celebrate its survival, Macau went on a building spree, erecting many of the city's stately homes and government palaces, as well as the Dom Pedro V Theatre, Military Club and later the Bela Vista Hotel.

Fortunately, Macau remained popular with foreigners who appreciated its faded charms. George Chinnery, doyen of China Coast artists, spent his last 27 years here (1825–52), recording the life of the ordinary people in watercolours and pen and pencil drawings, as well as depicting dignitaries in oils. The French artist Auguste Borget also made some memorable etchings during his sojourn here in 1838–39.

After concluding treaties with Britain, the United States and various European countries, China officially acknowledged the Portuguese presence for the first time in 1887 with the signing of a declaration that 'China confirms the perpetual occupation and government of Macau by Portugal'. At the same time, Taipa and Coloane islands were recognized as part of Macau, enlarging the territory to its present 17 square kilometres (6.7 square miles).

Since then, Macau's ability to survive against great odds has often been tested. In the 1930s the city almost starved when China embargoed vital supplies. During the Second World War, it remained neutral like Portugal, but opened its doors to tens of thousands of refugees from Hong Kong and Japanese-occupied China. Then in the 1960s it was rocked by shock waves from the Cultural Revolution in China.

In the 1970s the city entered a new age of prosperity, and today its factories earn about Ptc12 billion (US$1.5 billion) a year in exports and have a good reputation for high-quality garments, toys, electronics and other products. Tourism has also become big business, with an annual six million visitors, more than one million of whom are international arrivals; the rest are predominantly Hong Kong gamblers. Tourists who come in search of a four-century-old heritage are not disappointed. Historic buildings are in everyday use, traditional customs are alive and well, the churches and temples are busy and well-maintained, and there is something in the air that recalls an easy-going, rather rakish past.

On the other hand, there is plenty to suggest that Macau is a city on the move. Construction sites and new high-rises dominate the skyline, bright lights point the way to McDonald's and Pizza Hut, and work has begun on a US$835 million international airport to be built on reclaimed land.

The irony is that Macau, as we know it today, has a deadline it cannot avoid. Following the example of Hong Kong, the Portuguese have signed an agreement with China, which will resume sovereignty over Macau at midnight on 20 December 1999. After that, a certain amount of autonomy has been promised, but most of the territory's half a million people are not hopeful. Many are planning to emigrate, while the rest will remain in the first, and last, European outpost in Asia.

Don't call it a Colony!

Macau, derived from A-Ma-Gau or Bay of A-Ma in Chinese, was added by early settlers to the original title, giving the grand old name (in translation) of 'City of the Name of God, Macau. There is None More Loyal'. However, with its decline in fortunes, from the late 17th century it was usually described simply as a colony. Then in the 1950s Portugal integrated its foreign possessions by renaming them 'Overseas Portuguese Provinces'.

Following the Portuguese Revolution of 1974, Lisbon offered to hand Macau back to China. Peking declined, but Portugal decided to rename its last remnant of empire 'a Chinese Territory under Portuguese administration'. As a result, Macau is now generally referred to as a territory or enclave.

(The spelling 'Macao' is now outdated.)

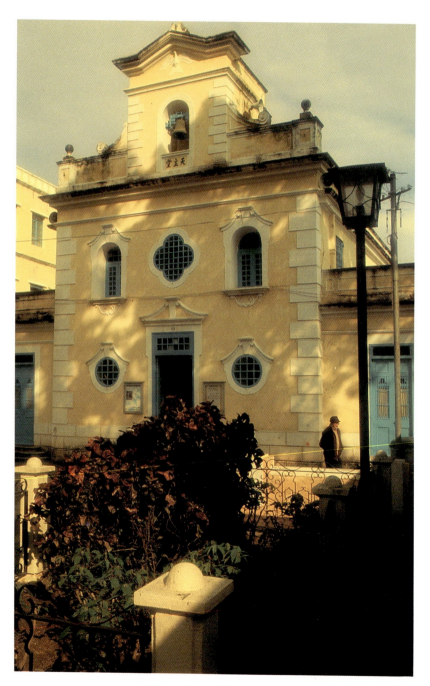

St Francis Xavier Church, Coloane

Facts for the Traveller

Getting There

If the international airport project proceeds as planned, visitors will be able to fly direct to Macau after 1995. Meanwhile, there is a **helicopter** service (except during bad weather) between Hong Kong and Macau, with at least eight round-trips a day. The flight takes 20 minutes and costs HK$982 on weekdays, HK$1082 on weekends and holidays. Telephone 859-3359 in Hong Kong, 572-983 in Macau. As for overland travel, a few tourists enter Macau from China, usually as part of a Hong Kong–Guangzhou–Macau triangular itinerary. However, for now, almost everyone arrives in Macau by sea from Hong Kong.

These arrivals now exceed six million a year—a daily average of almost 16,500! Most of them are casino-bound Hong Kong Chinese, but more than a million are foreign tourists. To cope with such numbers there is a large fleet of different vessels that make the 60-kilometre (40-mile) stretch of water between the colony and the enclave one of the world's busiest waterways.

Most vessels depart from the modern terminal in Shun Tak Centre, close to Hong Kong's Central district. A less frequent service is available from the new China Ferry Terminal in Kowloon. The Hong Kong Government charges a HK$22 departure tax and the Macau Government HK$20, both of which are usually included in the ticket price.

More than three-quarters of all travellers use the fleet of 16 Boeing **jetfoils**, which make the journey in 55–60 minutes. These are comfortable vessels, with snacks, drinks and telephones on board. Far East Jetfoils operates at least 68 daily round-trips from Shun Tak Centre: every 15 minutes on daytime services (7 am–5 pm); every 15–30 minutes until 1.30 am; and 2.30, 4.00 and 6.00 during the night. Fares range from HK$78 for weekday second class to HK$121 first class night service. Tickets can be purchased up to 28 days in advance at the terminal, at Ticketmate offices in Hong Kong MTR subway stations at Tsim Sha Tsui, Wan Chai, Causeway Bay and Mong Kok, and at Exchange Square, or by telephone (859-6596) using American Express, Diners Club, MasterCard and Visa cards. It is advisable to book early for holiday periods—and be sure to get return tickets at the same time.

The Hongkong Macao Hydrofoil Company operates a fleet of Swedish-built **jetcats**. There are 6 round-trips during daylight hours from the China Ferry Terminal in Kowloon, taking about 75 minutes. The company also operates 306-passenger **jumbocats**, which depart every 30 minutes from 8.00 am–5.30 pm, from Shun Tak Centre and take just over an hour. Fares are HK$70–88. Tickets are available at the terminals and by telephone (559-9255) using American Express, EPS, Fortune, FederalMaster and Visa cards.

Another way to bounce over the waves is by **hover-ferry**. There are 12 round-trips daily from the China Ferry Terminal in Kowloon between 8.30 am and late evening. Tickets, available at the terminal, are HK$60 on weekdays, HK$73 at weekends and HK$86 at night.

Visitors who prefer a more leisurely trip can take one of the two **high-speed ferries** which make the journey in about 100 minutes. These are ideal cruising craft, with comfortable seats, food and drink service, slot machines and sun decks. They make five or six round-trips a day, with departures from Shun Tak Centre between 8 am and 8 pm, returning from 10.30 am–10.30 pm. Fares are HK$30–62 on weekdays, HK$45–74 on weekends and Hong Kong holidays.

A word of warning! Be prepared for a certain amount of confusion at the Macau departure hall as people look for their gate. Also, the Hong Kong immigration halls are often very crowded.

Visas

Most people do not need a visa to enter Macau. Hong Kong Chinese don't even need a passport, only their Hong Kong Identity Card. Nationals of the United States and Canada, Britain and virtually all Western European countries, Japan, Thailand, the Philippines, Malaysia, Australia and New Zealand can stay without a visa for up to 20 days. Brazilians are given six months, while British Commonwealth subjects who are Hong Kong residents can stay up to 20 days.

Nationals of countries who have no diplomatic relations with Portugal must obtain visas from Portuguese consulates overseas, but everyone else can purchase a visa on arrival. For individuals they cost Ptc160, for children under 12 it is Ptc80, and for groups of ten or more, Ptc80 per person.

Customs

Apart from dangerous items there are no restrictions on goods or money brought into or taken out of Macau. (Hong Kong Customs limits foreign arrivals to a litre of alcohol and 200 cigarettes.)

Currency

Macau's unit of currency is the *pataca* (Ptc or sometimes MOP$), made up of 100 *avos*. It is virtually equivalent to the Hong Kong dollar, which circulates freely in Macau. As in Hong Kong, all foreign currencies and travellers' cheques are traded freely. There are international banks all over town, with those in the casinos open 24 hours a day.

Language

Portuguese is the official language, although only about three per cent of the population—mostly civil servants and old Macanese families—speak it. Cantonese is the native tongue of 95 per cent of all residents, with those whose jobs bring them into contact with foreigners (except taxi drivers) generally able to speak some English.

Communications

Macau has a new telephone system which offers fast, efficient communications within the territory and overseas. All local telephones and fax machines have international direct dialling, and there are plenty of public pay phones with IDD. However, in most hotels, guests have to go through the operator. The General Post Office provides a full range of postal services and staff speak English. There are also little red capsule post offices around town. Macau is well known among philatelists for its special stamp issues.

Climate and Clothing

Macau's climate is similar to that of Hong Kong, with hot, humid summers (May–September); dry, sunny autumns (October–December); changeable, chilly winters (January–April); and no discernible spring. Ties and jackets are virtually never required, and visitors should choose casual, comfortable, conservative clothing, and good walking shoes. As for the sudden shower or cold spell, there are plenty of cheap umbrellas and warm jackets.

Views of St Paul's past and present

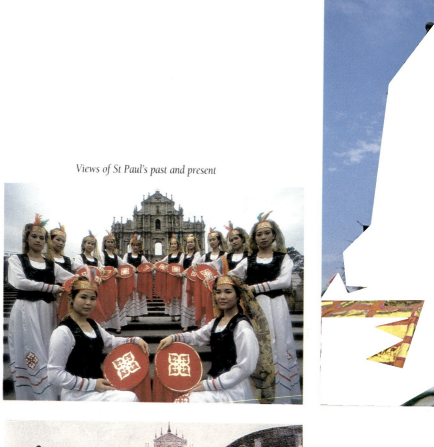

Month	Temperature						Relative Humidity	Rainfall
	Highest		Lowest		Mean			
	°C	°F	°C	°F	°C	°F	%	Inches
January	18.1	64.6	11.8	53.2	14.6	58.3	51	1.00
February	17.9	64.2	12.7	54.9	15.0	59.0	72	2.19
March	20.6	69.1	15.8	60.4	17.9	64.2	79	2.56
April	24.4	75.9	19.7	67.5	21.7	71.1	82	6.14
May	28.8	83.8	23.8	74.8	26.0	78.8	80	9.80
June	30.2	86.4	25.2	77.4	27.4	81.3	80	14.94
July	31.7	89.1	26.2	79.2	28.6	83.5	77	8.94
August	31.4	88.5	25.7	78.3	28.3	82.9	76	10.93
September	30.4	86.7	24.7	76.5	27.3	81.1	71	9.19
October	27.9	82.2	21.9	71.4	24.6	76.3	74	2.94
November	24.4	75.9	17.9	64.2	20.8	69.4	50	1.44
December	19.9	67.8	13.6	56.5	16.6	61.9	62	0.77

Public Holidays

Macau has the distinction of celebrating more Chinese festivals than China and more Portuguese *festas* than Portugal, with a few indigenous holidays added. Because Chinese festivals are celebrated according to the lunar calendar, the dates given below are approximate. For exact dates, consult the Macau Tourist Information Bureau. For details of festivals and other annual events, see Festivals of East and West (page 39–43).

January 1:	New Year's Day.
February/March:	First three days of Chinese New Year.
April:	Ching Ming (Sweeping of ancestral graves).
April 11:	Good Friday, Easter Monday.
April 25:	Anniversary of the 1974 Portuguese Revolution.
May 1:	International Labour Day.
May/June:	Dragon Boat Festival.
June 10:	Camões and Portuguese Communities Day.
June 24:	Feast of St John the Baptist.
August 15:	Feast of the Assumption.
September/October:	Mid-Autumn Festival.
October 1:	China's National Day.
October 5:	Portuguese Republic Day.

October: Cheung Yeung Festival.
November 2:   All Souls' Day.
December 1:   Restoration of Portuguese Independence.
December 8:   Feast of the Immaculate Conception.
December 22:   Winter Solstice.
December 24, 25:   Christmas.

Getting Around and Touring

The ideal way to explore Macau is on foot, but the ferry arrival terminal is *not* the place to set out because it is relatively distant from the most interesting areas. However, there are now several convenient modes of transport to take visitors from the wharf and around the territory.

Taxis are usually plentiful and most are airconditioned. The fare is Ptc6.50 for the first 1.5 kilometres (just under a mile), 80 avos for each subsequent 250 meters (274 yards). There is a Ptc5 surcharge for trips to Taipa and Ptc10 to Coloane (no surcharge on return trips). Few drivers speak English, so it is advisable to have your destination written in Chinese. Small change as a tip is welcome but not required. There is a new fleet of yellow cabs which you can order by telephone (337-711).

Public **buses** serve all parts of Macau from 7 am to 12 midnight for fares of Ptc1.50 in the city, Ptc2–3 to the islands. From bus stops at the wharf, routes 3, 3A and 10 go to the Lisboa Hotel, Sintra Hotel, Metropole Hotel, Avenida Almeida Ribeiro and the Inner Harbour; the 28C goes to the Lisboa, Royal Hotel and the border gate; while the 28A goes to the Hyatt Regency, Taipa village, Macau Jockey Club, New Century Hotel and Macau University. Itineraries in Portuguese are shown at bus stops, and most vehicles are quite comfortable (if sometimes crowded) and airconditioned (when the driver switches it on).

Pedicabs are the oldest surviving transport in Macau and well worth a trip, especially along the Praia Grande on a fine day. Fares are negotiable, but a single journey should not cost more than Ptc15. The pedicab drivers at the wharf usually demand Ptc40-plus for a short ride—and should not be encouraged in their greed.

It is also possible to pedal yourself, with **bicycles** available for hire from shops next to the Taipa bus terminal. Rates are Ptc8 per hour. Bicycles are no longer for hire in the city, where cycling is not the pleasure it can be on the islands.

However, for maximum freedom of the road, hire a **moke**. This is a runabout with the basic design of a small jeep, with detachable plastic side-panels and a retractable canvas roof. Mokes are easy and fun to drive, handling well on city streets and

Sixth-floor Paradise

We... drank warm gins and tonics under a banyan tree while I enlightened myself about the four Mr. Bigs—who, with the Portuguese government in the background, control pretty well everything that goes on in this enigmatic territory... The fortunes of these four gentlemen rose during and after the war—during the war, through trade with the Japanese who then occupied the mainland, and after the war, during the golden days when the harbour of Macao was thronged with ships from Europe smuggling arms to Communist China. Those latter days had turned Macao into a boom town when a single street running half the length of the town, the "Street of Happiness," had been one great and continuous street of pleasure and when the nine-story-high Central Hotel, the largest house of gambling and self-indulgence in the world, had been constructed ... to siphon off the cream of the pleasure-seekers. Those golden days had now passed. Communist China was manufacturing her own weapons, the Street of Happiness had emptied through lack of roistering sailors, and now pleasure, devoted only to the relaxation of Hong Kong tourists, was confined to the Central Hotel, whose function and design I recommend most warmly to the attention of those concerned with English morals.

The Central Hotel is not precisely a hotel. It is a nine-story skyscraper, by far the largest building in Macao, and it is devoted solely to the human so-called vices. It has one more original feature. The higher up the building you go, the more beautiful and expensive are the girls, the higher the stakes at the gambling-tables, and the better the music. Thus on the ground floor the honest coolie can choose a girl of his own class and gamble for pennies by lowering his bet on a fishing-rod contraption through a hole in the floor on to the gaming-tables below. Those with longer pocket can progress upwards through various heavens until they reach the earthly paradise on the sixth floor. Above this are the bedrooms. In the pursuit of information which would be in accordance with the readership of the Sunday Times, it was a matter of course that, very soon after our arrival at the Central Hotel, Dick Hughes and I should take the lift to the sixth floor.

Ian Fleming, Thrilling Cities

country trails. Drivers need to be at least 21 years old and hold an international licence or one recognized by Portugal.

There are two companies with fleets of mokes for hire by the day or weekend. Best known is Macau Mokes, which also has combination moke-hotel-restaurant packages. Their vehicles have candy-striped roofs and individual names. For information and bookings in Macau, telephone 378-851, fax 555-433; in Hong Kong, telephone 543-4190, fax 545-5626.

Avis Rent-a-Car offers mokes and cars. For information in Macau, telephone 555-686 ext 3004, fax 314-112; in Hong Kong, telephone 542-2189, fax 541-3254. International Tourism, the company with the Avis concession, also operates '**Tour Machines**'—small replicas of 1920s London buses, complete with leather-upholstered seating for nine and brass fittings. They can be hired for tours or transfers. (Contacts as for Avis.)

Tours are available from all Macau travel agencies (see Useful Addresses, page 127). They are real bargains, with prices kept low by the government. A half-day city tour covering all major attractions costs Ptc52–67 per person, depending on the number of passengers, and includes lunch. A two-hour tour across the bridge to the rural attractions of Taipa and Coloane islands costs Ptc10–15 per person by coach, Ptc160 for a party of four or less by car.

A new 30-minute tour takes the visitor to the Inner Harbour by **pleasure junk**. Operated by the Maritime Museum on Saturdays, Sundays and Mondays, the tour departs from Pier One four times a day. Tickets are Ptc10 from the museum.

Another tour provides a truly comprehensive view of Macau—from the air. The Macau Aero Club was formed in early 1990 by Taiwanese interests. Their craft are **ultra-light planes** that evoke the age of 'Those Magnificent Men in their Flying Machines'. Visitors can take ten-minute flights around the territory, at a low enough altitude for clear observation, at HK$300 per person. For information and bookings, call the Aero Club (307-343).

Entertainment

CASINOS
It has been labelled the Las Vegas or Monte Carlo of the Far East, but nobody goes to Macau's casinos for fabulous floor shows, free champagne or the chance of a mention in society columns. Most of the six million annual visitors come only to gamble, and must rank as the most dedicated gamblers in the world—whether housewives betting their last dollar or tycoons who boast as much about the millions they lose as those they win.

Gambling was legalized in Macau to provide a much-needed source of revenue after the British settlement of Hong Kong in 1841 reduced the Portuguese territory to a trading backwater. For over a century visitors came to try their luck at *fantan*, a game based on guessing the number of buttons on the table, and *dai siu* (large and small), where you wager on three dice.

Modern gambling had its beginning in 1962 when the gambling monopoly was awarded to the Sociedade de Turismo e Diversões de Macau (STDM, or 'the syndicate'), a group of local businessmen who contracted to build international casinos and hotels, provide transport from Hong Kong, keep the Outer Harbour dredged and pay a substantial amount in taxes. STDM has won every subsequent renewal of the franchise, (the current one extends beyond 1999!), and contributes about half of government revenue, as well as a lot of its tourism needs.

The number and quality of casinos has grown over the years, so that now there is gambling to suit every taste and wallet. The busiest and noisiest is located in a two-storey wing of the **Lisboa Hotel**. Open 24 hours a day, 365 days a year, it is regularly packed with punters playing blackjack, baccarat, boule, roulette, *fantan* and *dai siu*, or trying their luck at the hundreds of slot machines the Chinese call 'hungry tigers'.

The casino also has a computerized jackpot game, Pacapio. Whilst the games may look familiar to visiting gamblers, there are some Macanese variations. For instance at blackjack, anyone side-betting a larger amount than you can call your cards, and you might suspect, with some justification, that there is a conspiracy between some of the others at the table.

For details on these and other 'Macau rules', serious gamblers should look for a copy of *Gamblers Guide to Macau* by Bert Okuley and Frederick King-Poole, or *Macau Gambling Handbook* published by A-O-A, both available in Hong Kong.

In contrast to the Lisboa is the small, upmarket casino in the **Mandarin Oriental Hotel**. Also open 24 hours a day, it has blackjack, baccarat and *dai siu*, plus a slot machine room. It is rumoured that this is the choice venue for visiting high-rollers who prefer to remain incognito.

The **Taipa Diamond** in the Hyatt Regency is even more exclusive, being the only casino in town where US dollars alone may be used. Blackjack, baccarat and *dai siu* are played here, for very high stakes. There is also a special room with a US$10,000 minimum!

The newest casinos are in two of the most recently built hotels. There is a gaming hall in the **Kingsway**, catering to the average punter, while the casino in the **Westin Resort** is rather more up-market.

One of the special attractions of the slot machines in Macau is a 'Megabucks' system, whereby all the machines are linked to a jackpot that pays out millions of patacas to the occasional lucky gambler. To give their guests a chance to win such super pay-outs without going to a casino, the **Royal Hotel** has installed a slot machine hall, open 11 am–3 am.

There is also a separate machine hall in the huge casino on the ground floor of the **Jai Alai Stadium**. It is usually just as crowded as the main room, where gamblers wager their last dollars before leaving for Hong Kong from the wharf across the street. All games are available here and the casino is open 24 hours a day, every day of the year.

When ferries used the Inner Harbour (until the 1960s), these final flings took place in the **Macau Palace**, a triple-decker ferry converted into a colourfully ornate casino and restaurant moored next to the departure wharf. The original vessel was retired and replaced with a smaller but more salubrious, double-decker boat that had once served as a floating restaurant. Lavishly decorated with red and gold Chinese carvings, it tends to attract less affluent punters. One deck is full of slot machines and the other offers blackjack, baccarat and *dai siu*. It is open 24 hours a day.

Not far away, in a handsome old building on the main street, is the **Kam Pek casino**. Formerly housed in a dingy tenement, the casino was frequented mostly by locals; it now occupies two floors of bright, spacious halls with Western as well as Chinese games. It retains one local aspect in that all betting is done in patacas. (Hong Kong dollars are the currency of the other casinos.) Open 24 hours a day.

NIGHTCLUBS

Macau's nightclubs, like those in Hong Kong, cater primarily to local and visiting Chinese men. Other Asians who understand the hostess system if not the local language are also welcome. Westerners are warned that little English is spoken. However, the hostesses are pretty, and prices for drinks are well below those in Hong Kong.

The most expensive and sophisticated club is **China City**, a branch of the vast Hong Kong club of the same name. It is located on the second floor of the Jai Alai Stadium and is reached via a red carpet flanked with long-gowned hostesses who direct customers through a door to the club's escalator.

Open 6 pm to 4 am, it has a dance floor and a live band. The room is lit by tiny 'stars' in the ceiling and dimmed lamps on the low marble tables which are surrounded by deep couches. The hostesses, mostly Chinese, wear a variety of 'uniforms' from mini-skirts to harem pants and long, lacy dresses. Their companionship costs HK$30 per 12-minute unit. Drink prices rival those in five-star hotels, and there is a HK$200 minimum.

A new rival to the China City is the **Tonnochy Nightclub**, which is located in a downtown office building. It boasts elegant art deco furnishings, gorgeous hostesses, a dance floor and private karaoke lounges, one of them complete with its own dance floor. The minimum is HK$200.

The **Club Profiteer**, under the same management as the Tonnochy and in the same building, caters to the less exclusive market, with lower prices and less glamorous girls. In the same league is **Flower City**, situated on the Inner Harbour next to the floating casino. The latter has a HK$55 minimum.

The **Skylight** in the Presidente Hotel is more like a European nightclub. It has a stunning setting, being built on a terrace with glass walls that look out onto the Outer Harbour and a glass roof for star-gazing. Inside, the attractions are the pop music and a floor show performed by English strip-tease dancers. The Ptc48 admission charge includes one drink. Hours are 9 pm–4 am.

For those who enjoy a European-style dinner-dance (and have their own partner), the **Portas do Sol** in the Lisboa Hotel offer a superb dance floor and excellent music, with occasional performances of Portuguese folk dancing. Hours are 7 pm–1 am (2 am at weekends).

THE CRAZY PARIS SHOW

When STDM turned impresario in 1979 and launched a Parisian strip-show in the 19th-century Dom Pedro Theatre, few people believed it would become a popular staple on the Macau entertainment scene. At that time no one imagined that so many overseas tour operators would want to include a 'girlie show' on their itineraries, nor that by varying the programme, Hong Kong visitors would come back again and again.

Over the years, the numbers have become increasingly inventive, with music, costumes and sets to match the movements that are part ballet, part gymnastics. The cast changes constantly but generally includes girls from Australia, Britain, North and South America, and Europe.

The only number that does not change is 'The Mermaid', in which a dancer does a brilliant solo naked and underwater! The nudity is never objectionable, and women, who generally make up 40 per cent of the audience, enjoy it as much as the men.

There are nightly performances in the purpose-built Mona Liza Hall at the Lisboa at 8.30 pm and 10 pm, with an 11.30 pm show on Saturdays. Tickets (Ptc90–100) are available at all Macau hotels and travel agencies.

DISCOS

The karaoke craze has tended to usurp the disco market and there is no longer a pure discotheque in Macau. Instead, a combination of entertainment is offered, which includes disco music and lights along with karaoke lounges. The best of these is the **Prince Galaxie** in the New Century Hotel. It operates as a bar until the evening. There are no hostesses. Another good disco is found in the **Mondial Hotel**.

The Crazy Paris Show

Karaoke

The first sing-along bar in Macau was in the Japanese-managed **Royal Hotel**. Since then, karaoke lounges have appeared all over town.

Sauna and Massage

The 'flower houses' of the pre-war Macau, which earned a certain romantic notoriety, have been superseded by the ubiquitous massage parlour. Located all around town, they employ thousands of women from Thailand and the Philippines. Standards and prices vary; the deluxe venues are located in the Estoril, Lisboa, Presidente and Sintra hotels. Hours are from 12 noon to 4–6 am.

Sport

Horse Racing

The first European-style horse races on the China coast took place in Macau at the end of the 18th century. Organized by British merchants during the summers they spent in Macau between the Canton trading seasons, the meetings continued until the late 19th century; the area of the old track in the north of the city is still called by its original name, Extrada Marginal do Hipodromo.

Racing returned in 1980 with the opening of a trotting track on Taipa Island southwest of the bridge, a short ride from the Hyatt Regency Hotel. The facility, with an impressive four-storey grandstand and high-tech betting equipment, failed to make money and closed eight years later. But a group of investors, principally from Taiwan, decided there was a future for flat racing in Macau and formed the **Macau Jockey Club** (MJC). At a cost of HK$3,000 million (US$385 million), they rebuilt and extended the Taipa course, created a 1,400-metre (1,530-yard) all-weather track and a 1,576-metre (1,720 yard) grass track, installed an electronic tote system and huge video matrix screen, and built new quarters for up to 1,000 horses complete with airconditioned, muzak-fed stalls, a heated swimming pool and a horse hospital. The 18,000-seat grandstand was renovated and provided with a new race tower, weighing rooms, offices and VIP boxes.

Administrators, trainers, jockeys and vets were brought in from Britain, Ireland, Australia, New Zealand, France, Malaysia and Hong Kong; the horses are from Australia, New Zealand, Ireland and England.

Although the club had problems getting established, it now provides some excellent sport for visitors, with races twice a week during the September to June season. Daytime meetings begin at 2 pm, twilight events at 4.15 pm and night races at 7.30

pm. Overseas visitors can buy tickets at the track or at off-track betting centres, and information about schedules is available from the MJC offices on the third floor of Shun Tak Centre, Hong Kong (telephone 517-0872), or call 321-888 in Macau.

GREYHOUND RACING

Macau's canidrome, which opened in 1964 near the China border gate, is surrounded by multi-storey factories and apartment blocks on three sides and fortress-crowned Mong-Ha Hill on the other. It has seen tough times, but thanks to efficient management and professional trainers (mostly from Ireland and Australia) dog racing has become highly reputable and immensely popular, with local families as well as Hong Kong gamblers filling the stands.

Meetings of 14 races take place every Tuesday, Thursday and Saturday or Sunday, beginning at 8 pm and finishing a little after midnight. Entrance is Ptc2 and programmes cost Ptc5. Minimum bets are Ptcs2, with a full range of options such as quinellas and trifectas. Odds and results are shown on the big tote board. The races can also be watched on closed-circuit television in the Jai Alai Stadium, Lisboa Hotel and Kam Pek casino, where betting is available.

ROLLER-SKATING HOCKEY

The Macanese have a long history of playing field hockey and still compete with Hong Kong and other Asian teams. However, hockey on roller-skates is far more popular among young athletes.

The sport has long been a passion in Portugal and it was a Portuguese priest who introduced it to Macau in 1963.

Macau teams have entered many regional contests and won prizes and praise for their enthusiasm. This was one reason why Macau was chosen as the 1990 venue for the 24th World Roller-Skating Hockey Championships. Another reason was the opening of the Macau Forum, with its excellent playing arena. Contact the Tourist Office for more information.

GOLF

The new **Macau Golf and Country Club** is part of the Westin resort beside Hac Sa beach on Coloane Island. The clubhouse occupies the top three floors of the hotel, which is built into the headland. The 18-hole par-71 course was designed to championship standard by Aoki, the co-owner of the resort. Club facilities include sauna, jacuzzi and steambaths, massage rooms, a swimming pool, tennis courts, a veranda cafe and a large Japanese restaurant. For information about fees and availability for non-members call Hong Kong (852) 541-1812.

The Macau Grand Prix

Macau Grand Prix

Macau's annual Grand Prix is exciting and attracts an international field of drivers. As in Monaco, the races are held on city roads. The 6.1-kilometre (3.8-mile) Guia Circuit begins and ends on the straightaway along the Outer Harbour waterfront. It proceeds behind the Lisboa Hotel, past St Francis barracks, up Guia Hill to a series of turns that culminate in the Melco hair-pin before heading down to Fishermen's Bend and around the reservoir to the finish.

The Grand Prix takes place on the third or fourth weekend in November. It includes events for motorcycles, production cars and Formula Three models, plus races for veteran cars. Past winners of the Grand Prix, which began in 1954, include Alan Jones, Keke Rosberg, Riccardo Patrese, Geoff Lees and Ayrton Senna.

There are plenty of vantage points for watching the races around the circuit, but the best are the grandstand and the hotels on the Outer Harbour. Because hotel rooms are booked long in advance, Macau should be avoided at this time of year by anyone who isn't a race fan.

Macau Marathon

Since 1980, this event has attracted a growing number of runners. In 1989 the total topped 1,000. The route first circles the city, crosses the bridge, circles Taipa and Coloane islands and finishes back in town. Held early in December, it can be quite a gruelling exercise, but winners have clocked 2:18 hours. On the same day there is a shorter race for competitors in wheelchairs. For dates and information about entering, contact tourist information offices.

The Forum

The multi-purpose Forum provides Macau with a first-class venue for sporting events like **gymnastics, basketball** and **volleyball**, as well as international **table tennis** championships. The main hall can accommodate 4,000 spectators.

Other

Tennis and **squash** courts are available in the Hyatt Regency, Mandarin Oriental, New Century and Westin hotels, and there are ample opportunities for **jogging** in the city, over the bridge and around the islands. **Billiard halls** can be found in the Lisboa Hotel, Jai Alai Stadium and elsewhere; however, they are basically the preserve of local lads.

Cross-Cultural Cuisine

Macau has Chinese restaurants that rival those in Hong Kong, Japanese dining rooms on a par with Tokyo, authentic Portuguese food and Big Macs that are indistinguishable from those sold in Melbourne and Moscow.

Macanese cuisine developed from mix-matching ingredients and cooking methods from Europe, South America, Africa, India, Southeast Asia and China. Because Macau's melting pot dates back to the 16th century, the Macanese can lay claim to the first international cuisine.

One reason for this was Macau's position as both the culminating point of Portugal's worldwide empire and the gateway to China for the West. Other factors helped. For instance, Macau's settlers were merchants and priests who left such menial activities as farming and cooking to the Chinese.

As a result Macau benefited doubly—from the varied abundance of local farms and fisheries, and from the traditional expertise of Cantonese cooks, who quickly learnt to prepare European dishes using fast-frying techniques that seal in the flavour of the ingredients. In the early decades of contact with China, the Portuguese became the first Westerners to cook with ginger and soy sauce and the first to discover the laxative effect of rhubarb (creating a popular Chinese belief that the barbarians relied on it as their only diuretic!). They also ate lychees, and enjoyed the small local citrus so much that they had trees transplanted in Tangiers, where they became known as tangerines. As for drinks, the Portuguese adopted the Chinese habit of tea drinking in the 18th century and passed it along to visiting British traders.

In return, the Portuguese introduced various foodstuffs to China. From Brazil they brought peanuts, sweet potatoes and kidney beans; from Africa, *piri-piri* peppers; from India, chillies and shrimp paste; from the East Indies, pineapples and papayas; and from Europe, coffee, grape wine, green beans and lettuce. In some cases it is hard to determine who introduced what and to this day what Westerners call Chinese watercress is 'Portuguese vegetable' in Chinese.

While this culinary interchange enriched the diets of both East and West, it incidentally created the Macanese cuisine that can still be savoured today. It is by no means a regimented *haute cuisine*, but rather a pot-pourri of everyday dishes, some of them regular favourites, others created by experimentation with the vast range of available ingredients.

For truly authentic Macanese food you must either eat with a Macanese family or visit the Riquexo Restaurant. Here you will find *minchi*, a dish of minced pork and diced potatoes pan-fried in soy; duck baked in its own blood with Chinese greens; and a stir-fried stew of chicken, beef, pork, prawns and vegetables in a sauce of lemon, soy, laurel and chilli known as Macanese '*arroz gordo*' (literally 'fat rice').

There are other Macanese dishes that appear on the menus of many Portuguese or continental restaurants. Try the popular African chicken, baked or roasted in *piri-piri* and chilli peppers, or its equally fiery cousin, Goanese chicken. Spicy prawns are another favourite, with every kitchen boasting its own recipe for the hot sauce that accompanies the giant prawns caught in local waters.

One dish that illustrates Macau's status as a culinary crossroads is the mis-named Portuguese chicken. It consists of chunks of chicken baked with potatoes, tomato, olive oil, curry, coconut, saffron and black olives.

The Chinese and Portuguese share a sweet tooth, so there are always banana fritters and fruit-filled pancakes on the menu. Among typical Macanese creations are pumpkin and fig compote, mango mousse, and a *batatada* of potatoes, eggs and coconut.

Alongside these delights, mention should be made of a Chinese eating custom that many Westerners find abhorrent—the consumption of wild animals such as civet cats and owls. Many of these creatures are officially protected by Portugal and China, but this doesn't stop their being imported live and exhibited in cages outside some restaurants. The Chinese see no difference between this custom and Westerners' cooking of domesticated animals.

Shopping

There are basically two categories of people who come to shop in Macau—antique collectors and bargain hunters from Hong Kong. The former are less numerous than in years past, when they were more likely to discover treasures among the trash. For one thing, antique shop owners know the market value of their wares. For another, there are fewer valuable antiques coming onto the Macau market, due in part to the exodus of Macanese families who often sold off their heirlooms before they left.

The other source is China, but the ban on illegal exports means that the goods smuggled in tend to be small or easily portable items. These continue to lure collectors and dealers, who regularly do the rounds in search of fresh arrivals from over the border.

As in Hong Kong, the vast majority of merchandise on offer is Qing-Dynasty chinoiserie: polychrome porcelain vases, ornate figurines, elephant-shaped stools, heavy blackwood furniture and intricately embroidered screens. This oriental Victoriana is still very popular with the Chinese, although much of it is of dubious investment value. Westerners and Japanese, on the contrary, are more likely to seek out

Traditional Chinese wine shop

(above) *Different varieties of rice on sale in open-fronted stores;*
(below) *gold is bargain-priced in Macau*

older items, such as undecorated Ming ceramics that were once used as ships' ballast, ancient coinage in the shape of knives, classic scroll paintings, old jade and unusual snuff bottles.

Recommended antique shops are **Veng Meng** (114 Ave de Almeida Ribeiro and 8 Travessa do Pagode), **Wing Tai** (1A Ave de Almeida Ribeiro), **Hong Hap** (133 Ave de Almeida Ribeiro) and **The Antique Shop** (11 Ave de Coronel Mesquita, opposite Kun Iam Temple). There are also several shops on Rua de São Paulo, below the church ruins, where good antiques can occasionally be found among the souvenirs, folk art and modern reproductions. Most shops have English-speaking staff and accept major credit cards. Although antiques are probably cheaper in Macau than in Hong Kong, they are not the bargains that attract residents of that 'shoppers' paradise'. For them the prime lure is gold—in the form of 24-carat jewellery at the world's lowest prices. Like Hong Kong, Macau imports the precious metal (and precious stones) duty-free and sells it at the international commodity rate. In Hong Kong, however, high overheads have to be paid. In Macau, the price for 24-carat gold is determined by its weight in taels (the Chinese measure equivalent to 1.2 troy ounces) and each of the hundreds of jewellery shops displays the daily (or hourly) London gold price in taels. A small processing fee is added.

The Chinese buy such ornaments principally as an investment. For those seeking adornment, the shops sell 18-carat jewellery set with diamonds, rubies, emeralds, pearls and other gems, all at remarkably low prices. Staff are far more friendly and helpful than in Hong Kong. English is widely spoken, credit cards are accepted and most shops stay open until mid-evening.

Some of the best are found on the Avenida de Almeida Ribeiro and include **Tai Fung** at number 36, **Chow Sang Sang** at 58 and **Pou Fong** at 91.

Bargains of another kind are found in the street stalls, where the over-runs and seconds from local garment factories are sold for a few patacas. Some are clever fakes, but many of the garments with big fashion labels are genuine, because the likes of Yves St Laurent, Cacharel, Adidas and Gloria Vanderbilt have their clothes made here under licence.

There are plenty of shops selling these sweaters, jeans, shirts and sportswear (in a wide range of sizes), but the best prices are found at stalls off Leal Senado Square next to São Domingos market and along Rua Cinco de Outubro.

Another good source of bargains are the pawnshops that flourish in the shadow of the casinos. The *casas de penhores* offer some incredible buys in barely-used cameras, gold watches and jade. Most of the items are genuine—as befits shops with names like Honesty and Sincerity—but be warned that you have no legal recourse if you buy a fake. Pawnshops are open until late at night and are distinguished not by the familiar sign of three balls but by a stylized gourd.

Festivals of East and West

Although many holidays in Macau are celebrated by the locals as days off or occasions for private devotion, there are some that can be observed and enjoyed by foreign visitors. In addition there are a growing number of annual events of special or general interest.

Chinese New Year (the beginning of the lunar year, occuring between late January and late February) is very much a family affair and usually not a good time to visit Chinese cities. In Macau, however, there are public spectacles, including a magnificent flower market in the sports ground behind the Lisboa, Cantonese opera performed on bamboo stages, special exhibitions and big-prize dog races.

At this time of year, traditional shops sell strips of lucky red paper inscribed with auspicious Chinese characters, which are posted up around every front door, sometimes with new pictures of guardian door gods, while inside each home old pictures of the kitchen god are ceremonially burnt and replaced with new ones.

The new year itself is welcomed in with the roar of endless strings of firecrackers. Then, having scared away the evil spirits, people visit their relatives, eat sumptuous meals, put on new clothes and pay their respects at the temples.

Only those engaged in essential services work during the first three days of the lunar new year, and some professions—such as carpenters and printers—take off ten days or more. On the 15th day of the lunar year, the **Lantern Festival** is celebrated, when families gather for picnics in the parks under the full moon, with candle-lit lanterns shaped like animals, boats, aeroplanes or spaceships.

East and West come together to celebrate springtime, bringing colour and pageantry to Macau. The community of devout Catholics prepares for Easter with the **Procession of Our Lord of Passos**, but unlike everywhere else in the world, on the first day of Lent instead of Good Friday. The image of Christ bearing the cross is carried from the Cathedral on the shoulders of purple-cloaked dignitaries to its home church of St Augustine via stations of the cross set up across town. Leading the parade are the clergy in crimson and white, representatives of religious congregations holding heraldic banners, a young woman playing the role of Veronica and the police band. They are followed by crowds of local people, both Christian and non-Christian, who join together in a centuries-old ritual.

Easter coincides with the third lunar month, when two popular Chinese festivals are celebrated. **Ching Ming** is a time to sweep and decorate family graves, before sharing a feast of roast suckling pig with the ancestral spirits.

A week later the seafarers' goddess who gave Macau its name, **A-Ma**, is honoured. The original temple and others dedicated to Tin Hau (another version of her name)

(following pages) *International Fireworks Festival over the Macau–Taipa Bridge*

attract huge crowds of devotees who bring offerings of food and joss sticks. Fishermen stay in port, their junks festooned with coloured banners, and on stages in the street there are performances of Cantonese and Chiu Chow opera.

Mid-summer is another time for varied festivities. The most exciting for visitors as well as residents is the **Dragon Boat Festival**, on the fifth day of the fifth moon, which falls sometime in June. Macau's fishing communities decorate their boats, set off firecrackers and compete against each other and teams from abroad in dragon boats—long narrow canoes bearing dragon heads and tails.

Praia Bay is a natural amphitheatre for the annual extravaganza, the **Fireworks Festival**, with different countries (including Japan and China) showing off their pyrotechnic skills on a series of summer nights. The fireworks are launched from a site in front of the Lisboa and can be seen from thousands of vantage points along the praia. For details of dates, contact offices of the Macau Tourist Information Bureau.

More goes up in smoke in the middle of the seventh moon (August or early September) during the **Festival of the Hungry Ghosts**. Devotion to one's ancestors is a basic tenet of traditional Chinese communities, and few are more devout than in Macau, where families ensure their forebears are buried with due ceremony and then supplied during the long years of purgatory with burnt offerings of large-denomination 'hell banknotes' and paper houses, furniture, cars, servants and other comforts.

During the Hungry Ghosts festival, however, the stacks of paper gifts are offered not to family members but to the disadvantaged souls of those who died without kin or proper burial. The Chinese believe that at this time of the year, these ghosts roam the earth seeking revenge for their misery by making trouble. The gifts are to placate them, as are special opera performances and prayers. At the culmination of the festival a 4.5-metre- (15-foot-) tall *papier-mâché* effigy of Daai Si, the custodian of hell, is paraded through the streets before being sent home in smoke, along with the ghosts.

The emphasis shifts from hell to heaven during the eighth moon—the harvest moon in the West—which waxes on the 15th day to mark the **Mid-autumn**, or **Mooncake Festival**. People celebrate with lanterns, many in the shape of the rabbit who lives on the moon concocting the elixir of immortality, and with picnics in the parks, ideally under a clear sky and brilliant moon.

Mooncakes are an essential part of the occasion. They are made of ground lotus seeds or red beans sometimes baked with as many as four duck egg yolks surrounded by heavy dough. They commemorate the 14th-century anti-Mongol rebellion when Chinese conspirators communicated among themselves by means of secret messages concealed in the cakes. The revolt succeeded, which is probably why mooncakes are today considered lucky (if rather indigestible).

Heavenly delights of another kind are on hand in October during the week-long **Music Festival**, which attracts some outstanding international artists. The programme includes concerts of choral and orchestral works, solo recitals and chamber ensembles, with at least one choral concert held in the evocative setting of a baroque church, and many chamber events taking place in the pavilion of the Lou Lim Ieoc Garden.

In addition, Macau stages an annual **Jazz Festival**, with visiting artists who have performed in such venues as the Lou Lim Ieoc Garden. Dates and artists tend not be finalized until the last moment, so jazz fans should check with Macau Tourist Information Bureau offices. (MTIB also has current dates for festivals based on the lunar calendar.)

Museums, Art Galleries and Archives

Macau can no longer be called a living museum, although in places it has the makings of a historical movie set. The city has many buildings that could well house specialized museum collections.

For many years some of Macau's best archeological, historical and artistic treasures were gathered together in the Camões Museum. This name applied to the 18th-century mansion beside the Camões Gardens that once served as the home away from home for committee presidents of the British East India company and provided lodging for visiting ambassadors. The museum was closed in 1989 and totally rebuilt in the original style, but with all modern conveniences. In 1991, it was reopened as the **Casa Garden** and is the local office of the Orient Foundation. Three rooms are used to display the museum collection of Chinese porcelain, Buddhist art and Exportware (open during working hours). In the basement is an art gallery for regular exhibitions of paintings, photography and sculpture (open daily 9.30 am–6 pm). There is also a small theatre for films, recitals and jazz concerts.

The **Maritime Museum** is an outstanding example of a new museum in an ideal location. It occupies a building designed to suggest stylized sails, which stands next to Wharf Number One and opposite the A-Ma Temple, that is virtually on the spot where the Portuguese first landed. Surprisingly, this is the first museum in Asia devoted to the sea. Part of the collection focuses on the fishing industry, which is common throughout the region. Exhibits include traditional fishing gear, a working sampan, lighted maps of the fishing grounds for different species, ocean-going shrines and paper boats burnt in offerings and such local curiosities as a wooden sled on which shrimp catchers skim across the mud-flats of Praia Grande Bay at low-tide.

Another section of the museum is dedicated to the journeys of two outstanding explorers—Vasco da Gama and the 15th-century Chinese admiral, Cheng Ho (Zheng He). Lights show their routes, copies of their charts cover the walls and models of their ships—made by the master craftsman Vasco of Lisbon—are on display. Here also are samples of their cargoes and the equipment they carried, including early Chinese compasses and axial rudders, together with European astrolabes and knotted flax lines used to measure nautical speed.

In addition, the museum features vessels from later periods, including a pirate war junk, a Portuguese *lorcha*/pirate-chaser, and some of the coastal steamers which used to ply between Macau and Canton. Among other relics is a paraffin lamp from the Guia lighthouse.

There are two specially constructed set pieces that bring old Macau into sharp focus. One is a television-style light box illustrating the story of A-Ma. The other is a bas relief of Macau as it was in the 17th century, in the city's golden age.

Model in the Maritime Museum

One of the museum's designers came up with an idea as inspired as it was obvious: to use the wharf for real-life, floating exhibits! These include a tugboat, a fishing junk, a *lorcha* and one of the dragon boats raced during the Dragon Boat Festival.

(The museum is open daily, except Tuesdays, from 10 am to 6 pm. There is an admission charge of Ptc5.)

The **Taipa House Museum** is an authentic middle-class Macanese home of the early 20th century. It is one of a dignified row of pastel-green and white-stucco houses dating from the 1920s. It looks out over the banyan-shaded praia of Taipa village on to a bay which was once an anchorage for tea clippers. (The museum is open daily, except Mondays, from 9.30 am–1.00 pm, and 3.00pm–5.30pm.)

The **Post Office Museum** is a new attraction for anyone interested in the development of communications in Asia over the past century. The two floors of the museum, linked by a spiral staircase, are tucked into one corner of the General Post Office on Avenida de Almeida Ribeiro.

Unfortunately, the catalogue and labels are in Portuguese and Chinese only, but enthusiasts should have few problems identifying the exhibits. Macau's maritime post was established in 1800, but it wasn't until 1884 that it became a public service, thanks to the introduction of adhesive stamps.

These and later stamp issues are displayed on the upper floor of the museum, where philatelists can see such rarities as 1910 stamps with pictures of the assassinated King Carlos overprinted with 'Republica' and the royal word for cents, *reis*, blacked out.

Macau's first post office was opened in 1885 by Ricardo de Sousa, the first postmaster general, in his home on the Praia Grande. This became a postal hub for the Pearl River estuary, as illustrated by the collection of ivory-handled chops marked with such destinations as Kongmoon and Heungshan, plus those designating outbound mail to Europe via Siberia or America by packet boat.

Other post office equipment on display includes large wooden abacuses, an early post-box and a postman's bicycle. They share space with specimens of some original telecommunications equipment—such as the earliest telephones, the first telex machines and a 1930s Siemens automatic central exchange (still in working order).

The Department of Posts, Telephone and Telegraph (CTT) moved into the present building in 1931. Two years later the territory made its first broadcasts on Radio Macau. The station, which went on the air only two or three times a week, now occupies a corner of the museum, complete with massive turntables, a Pathé News microphone and a 600-watt transmitter.

(The Post Office Museum is located on the second floor of the GPO building, accessible from the side door. It is open on weekdays 3–5 pm, or by arrangement with CTT.)

The **Memorial Home of Sun Yat-sen** cannot compare with the museums devoted to the revolutionary hero in his birthplace, Cuiheng, and elsewhere in China, but it is an interesting side-show for admirers of the doctor-scholar who led the 1911 Revolution that overthrew the Manchu Empire and gave birth to the Chinese Republic.

Sun had graduated from college in Hong Kong and medical school in Canton before he arrived in Macau to work at Kiang Vu Hospital. It was 1892, and the young man was fired with ideas of democracy and Christianity which he had been exposed to as a teenager in Honolulu. Now he was determined to reform China's backward society. During the two years he worked in Macau, he wrote newspaper articles advocating reform and held meetings with like-minded Chinese.

The authorities in Peking, not surprisingly, tried to silence him. They sent agents to Macau, forcing Sun to flee and continue his work in Europe, Japan and the United States, while his first wife and their children stayed in Macau. His original house burned down in the 1930s and was replaced with the present building.

Located at Rua Ferreira do Amaral 1, not far from the Estoril Hotel, it sports a façade of pseudo-Arabic arches and candy-twist columns that make an incongruous setting for the red and gold Chinese name plaque over the door. The collection inside is somewhat haphazard and neither well-lit nor adequately labelled. Most of the exhibits are photographs and press clippings of Sun's life as a revolutionary on the run and, after 1911, as an elder statesman in China. There are also some original Kuomintang flags, furniture from the old house and first editions of Sun's works.

(The Sun Yat-sen Memorial Home is open 10 am–1 pm daily except Tuesdays, and 3–5 pm on weekends.)

There is no city art gallery in Macau, but plenty of **art exhibitions**. The most imaginative venue is the **Leal Senado Gallery**, which was converted from offices next to the entrance foyer of the Loyal Senate. The two large rooms with high ceilings and good lighting provide an excellent showcase for travelling exhibitions, retrospectives and displays by local painters, sculptors and photographers. The foyer is also sometimes used. There is little advance notice of exhibitions, but you can check with tourist information offices in Hong Kong and Macau.

Another venue for exhibitions that come and go with little fanfare is the pavilion in the **Lou Lim Ieoc Garden**. A special Chinese New Year exhibition is held here, featuring the animal of the year as well as periodic displays of such things as Chinese ethnic costumes and scroll paintings. Check first with the tourism offices, but be sure to include the pavilion in a visit to the garden.

Visitors who want to delve deeper into Macau's history have plenty of opportunities. This isn't to say that it is easy—odd hours and disorganized cataloguing don't help—but a vast amount of material is available.

Iland of Macao

Macao standeth at one end of a greatt Iland built on rising hills, some gardeins and trees among their houses making a pretty prospecte somwhatt resembling Goa, allthough not soe bigge; Their houses double tyled, and thatt plaistred over againe, for prevention of Hurracanes or violentt wyndes that happen some Yeares, called by the Chinois Tuffaones, which is allso the reason (as they say) they build no high towers Nor steeples to their Churches.

Ilands about Macao

Beeffore Macao are many Ilands, some greater some lesse some inhabited, most part nott; high uneven land, no trees, much grasse and plenty of water springs; very stony, many great ones such as wee have in some part off the Westcountry, called Moorestones; Many China vessells passing to and Fro, none coming near us except the aforementioned Watche [guard] boates or some other with the Governours leave.

In whatt the Portugalls att Macao Doe take Delightt in, with their recreationes

All the recreations of this Citty ly within themselves, As their faire large strong Ritche and well furnished houses, Their wives and Children as Ritche in Jewells and apparell, their Number off slaves (For the most part the Men slaves Curled head Caphers and the Femalles Chinesas), Their meetings, Feastings and rejoycings att their weddings, Christnings and holidaies (which are often); having Neither Fields Nor gardeins abroad, the Chinois not allowing them.

A straunge plantt

Some trees are to bee seene here and there in the Citty and some smalle gardein plottes, butt in their houses Many galleries and tarasses Furnished with Macetas, or Flower potts, made into sundry shapes, wherein were various sorts of smalle trees, plantts, Flowers, etts. Among the rest a smalle tree (common here) growing outt off a Meere rocke or stone, which is putt into a panne or other vessell off water, soe that the water cover the roote and some part off the stocke, and soe it waxeth greater, having seene some off 3 or 4 Foote high.

This "strange plant" was identified by C M Jame as being Narcissus Tazetta or shui-sin-fa, "water fairy flower" in Cantonese.

Peter Mundy, 1637

Early map of Macau, Wattis Fine Art

For serious scholars, the **Historical Archives** is a treasure-house of books, letters and manuscripts pertaining to the Portuguese explorations, Catholic missions in Asia, diplomatic embassies and the history of China, Japan and Southeast Asia from the 16th to 19th centuries. The most valuable manuscripts, including 7,500 items dating from 1587 to 1786, are on microfilm and there are experienced staff to help locate specific information. The archives are housed in one of a row of restored colonial mansions on Avenida de Conselheio Ferreira de Almeida. (It won a Pacific Area Travel Association Heritage Award in 1982.) Visitors are welcome during working hours: 9.30 am–5.30 pm on weekdays, 9.30 am–5 pm on Saturdays.

Those interested in Macau's history during the last century, as well as the Western experience in China, should allocate some afternoon hours to the library situated at the top of the stone staircase in the **Leal Senado**. It contains bound copies of local newspapers from as early as the 1820s and documents relating to Timor and other parts of the former Portuguese empire.

Most visitors, however, will head for the collection of rare books on China kept in the old part of the library. This was built by local craftsmen following the model of the Mafra Convent library in Portugal. Its carved panels, staircases and balconies are made of teak, which not only looks beautiful but helps to preserve the books from insects and mould.

Here you will find one of the most comprehensive collections of 19th- and early 20th-century English-language books about China in the world. They were inherited by the library after the Second World War from the old Lappa Customs Office, which had been run for a century by mostly British officers who lived with their families in Macau and gathered just about everything ever written about China. This includes travellers' diaries, missionaries' biographies, romantic novels and learned papers on every conceivable aspect of the country and its people—from the entomology of the Gobi Desert to the speech patterns of Yangtze boatmen and the origins of the Taiping Rebellion.

The library is open Monday to Saturday from 1 to 7 pm, however, the stacks where the older newspapers are held are not open until 3 pm.

Sights

Being small and compact, Macau should be easy to explore, but it is not. The problem stems from four and a half centuries of casual construction and the variable capacity for survival of the buildings and the institutions they housed.

The result is a historical jigsaw, wherein a 19th-century colonial house can share a city block with a one-room textile factory, a high-rise bank and the neighbourhood Taoist shrine. It might sound chaotic, but in fact it follows a pattern that makes sense in Macau where every place serves a purpose.

The Portuguese enclave shares a history with other Western trading posts in Asia. Colonial mansions, churches, clubs, concert halls and other evidence of European culture can be found throughout the region, superimposed on an alien, oriental world. But only in Macau do so many heritage buildings survive and play a role in the daily life of the people.

In recent years a conservation movement has grown up, resulting in many outstanding renovation projects, some of which have won international heritage awards. Historically, however, buildings were preserved because there was no money to replace them with something modern. Unfortunately, more funds are now available and the evidence of progress is increasingly distorting the skyline and overshadowing, but not diminishing, the monuments of the past.

The major sightseeing districts are around St Paul's, on Penha peninsula, in the residential parish of St Lazarus and on the offshore islands. Conducted tours include the most famous sights and visitors with sufficient time can explore further independently. (The Tourist Office has a brochure describing walking tours.)

Chinese Ancestry - Temples and Shrines

The beliefs, arts and customs of traditional China thrive in Macau, where a devout, conservative community somehow manages to compete in the rat race while meeting their obligations to their ancestors and gods.

Although they are labelled Buddhist or Taoist, most of Macau's worshippers revere deities from both religions, as well as a few animist spirits. There is nothing too strange about this because both Buddhism (with the Buddhist trinity and attendant *bodhisattvas* like the Goddess of Mercy, Guanyin or Kun Iam) and Taoism (with its pantheon of immortalized humans, such as A-Ma, Goddess of the Sea, and Guan Di or Kwan Tai, the God of Wealth, Literature, War and Pawnshops) preach the sanctity of life, devotion to the gods and reverence for the ancestors.

Most of the temples, or *miu*, comfortably accommodate images from both religions. Many also contain two imposing guardians: axe-bearing Thousand-*li* Eye, who can see forever, and club-wielding Favourable Wind Ear, who can hear everything. In addition, there are gods in charge of each year and others that serve the needs of girls seeking husbands, women wanting sons, students taking exams and desperate gamblers.

There are no set hours of worship, except for funerals and festivals. Otherwise people drop by at any time to offer a prayer, ask a favour or give thanks. The temples (solely supported by devotees) are open all day and evening. They are maintained by a caretaker, who makes a living from selling joss sticks (the spiral incense 'chandelier' suspended from the ceiling burns for two weeks) and interpreting fortune sticks called *chim* which you shake from a round container.

The priests, who usually reside on the premises, earn their living from commissioned prayers for the dead and the sale of paper houses, furniture, cars and 'hell banknotes', which are ceremonially burnt at funerals to make the after-life more comfortable for the departed.

Visitors are welcome to inspect the temples, as long as they show proper respect, and photography is allowed, particularly if you contribute to the caretaker's 'oil money' box. In addition to the statues, an altar laden with the five ritual vessels (incense burner, two candlesticks and two flower vases), brocade banners and memorial calligraphy, Westerners are usually attracted to the traditional architecture. Dominant are the high-raked roofs of semi-circular tiles, their ridge-poles bristling with porcelain dragons and other auspicious symbols and their eaves decorated with intricately carved friezes.

The interior consists of prayer halls, funeral chapels and open courtyards containing bronze censers for burnt offerings. Ceilings are of dark wooden beams and white plaster tiles. Some temples also have gardens with sacred trees, bamboo groves and occasionally a vegetarian restaurant.

The **A-Ma Temple** is a prime sight, scenically and symbolically. Situated at the entrance to the Inner Harbour, it marks the birthplace of Macau as a settlement long before the Portuguese arrived. According to legend, a poor girl from a fishing village sought free passage along the coast. The rich junk owners refused her, but a small fishing boat took her on board. Out at sea, a typhoon struck and all the vessels except the fishing boat she was on were lost. The boat landed on a small peninsula at the mouth of the Pearl River, and the girl revealed herself to be A-Ma, Goddess of Seafarers, who is also known as Tin Hau. In her honour, the fishermen built a temple on the spot where they had safely come ashore.

More prosaically, it is known that when fishermen from Fujian Province on the east coast of China settled here in the 15th century, they built a temple to their

Old Temple Near the Entrance to Macau by Auguste Borget (1839)

patron goddess. When the Portuguese arrived in 1555, they learned that the name of the place was A-Ma-Gau, or Bay of A-Ma. When, two years later, the Westerners came to stay, Lisbon christened it City of the Name of God in China (Cidade do Nome de Deus de Macao na China), but the early settlers preferred their version of the local name, Macau.

Over the centuries the temple has been richly endowed and regularly renovated by its devotees. It has also attracted many generations of visitors, including the artist Auguste Borget, who portrayed it in his famous lithographs.

The pictorial appeal is just as obvious today, and despite the modern buildings on the reclaimed waterfront, the temple retains its harmony with nature. The Chinese remark on its good *fung shui*: it is geomantically well-sited, with its back to the hill (where protective dragons dwell) and its front gate facing the sea.

The temple has four shrines built into the boulder-strewn hillside. The lower three are dedicated to A-Ma and her attendants, Kam Tung (Golden Boy), Yok Noi (Jade Maiden), Tei Chong Wong (King of Hell) and Wai To (Protector of the Law). The uppermost shrine belongs to Kun Iam (Guanyin), the Buddhist Goddess of Mercy.

The shrines are linked by paths that wind through moon gates and between rocks carved with red Chinese characters. These quote the scriptures or are eulogies to A-Ma. One says, 'Macau is under her protection and the place is beautiful'; another reads, 'Because of her virtue, ships can sail safely on the oceans like sea-birds in fine weather'.

The most famous carving is on a boulder in the entrance courtyard. It shows the boat (remarkably similar to a Portuguese sailing ship of the same era) which carried A-Ma, etched in bright colours that are renewed annually. On the stern is a banner inscribed, 'Safely crossed the great river'.

Another interesting feature is a grove of giant bamboo next to the uppermost shrine. The bamboos are festooned with twists of fortune papers and small dolls, placed there by women hoping to bear children. Nearby is a fine little belvedere, with stone seats and a lovely view of temple roofs and Lappa Island, across the busy harbour in China. Lappa Island, a former burial site for Jesuit priests, was once a favourite picnic area for Macau residents and tourists. There is a lion dance performance in front of the temple at 10 am every Sunday and public holiday, lasting 30 minutes.

The **Kun Iam Temple** is possibly the oldest institution in Macau. It is said to have been founded in the 13th century by a community of Cantonese farmers, however, the present structures date from 1627. The temple is purely Buddhist, with the first prayer hall devoted to the Three Precious Buddhas—Sakyamuni (the founder of Buddhism), the Lord of the Western Paradise, and the Medicine Buddha. The second hall, with an open courtyard, contains an image of the Buddha of Longevity.

Beyond is the main hall, dedicated to Kun Iam, whose statue, in embroidered silk with a beaded veil, occupies an altar draped with gorgeous brocade. According to one legend, the goddess was a princess who defied her father by entering a convent. He had it burnt down, but she escaped, and he was so angry he had her executed. She went to hell, but her presence turned it into heaven, so she returned to earth where she cured her father of a fatal disease and converted him and his kingdom to Buddhism.

This story is told in classic Chinese calligraphy on hanging scrolls in the temple's spacious antechamber, where funeral services and prayer meetings are held. Part of this temple's obvious wealth comes from VIP funerals and the sale of paper offerings, which can often be seen here.

The prime tourist attraction, however, has nothing to do with religion or art. It consists of a round stone table in the temple garden, together with a marble plaque inscribed in Chinese. It records the historic occasion on 3 July 1844 when the Viceroy of Canton, Kiying (Qiying), and Caleb Cushing, Envoy Extraordinary and Minister Plenipotentiary of the United States, signed the first **Sino-American treaty** here.

It was described in Washington as a friendship pact, but was actually forced upon the Chinese because American traders wanted the same access to China's ports as the British had won three years before as a result of the First Opium War. The only concession to face was having the treaty signed in Macau rather than on Chinese soil. (Cushing rented a house in Macau which served as the US Consulate for China until 1885, when an embassy was opened in Peking.)

In addition to the 'treaty table', the temple gardens are worth exploring. They rise into the slopes of Guia Hill, with landscaped terraces, omega-shaped graves, bamboo groves, simple earth shrines, plaster birds, and the 'Sweetheart Tree', actually four ancient banyans whose branches are intertwined, symbolizing true love.

The temple is located on Avenida do Coronel Mesquita, in the northern suburbs. Special festivities are held here four times a year, on the 19th day of the second, sixth, ninth and eleventh moons.

The **Lin Fong Miu**, or Lotus Temple, is not as well known among visitors as it should be. One problem is its location, at the busy intersection of Avenida Almirante Lacerda and Estrada do Arco. With the constant traffic at the nearby border gate, heavy trucks serving the neighbouring industrial areas and punters on their way to the nearby greyhound track, the temple has a rather desolate and undistinguished appearance.

But once in the small courtyard, you will appreciate why Lin Fong is cited as one of the treasures of Macau. The major reason is its façade of bas-relief clay friezes. They cover the eaves and lintels with intricate tableaux depicting flowers and birds, symbols of good fortune and—most brilliantly—groups of people who seem to be

(above) *A-Ma Temple*; (below) *offerings of joss sticks*; (right) *lion dancers*

engaged in lively conversation. They were fashioned in the 19th century in workshops near Canton and in 1980, when the temple was extensively renovated. During this renovation the interior was stripped down. Under centuries of accumulated candle and incense smoke were revealed fine ceilings with the original teak beams. The faded banners, tattered paper offerings and general grime was removed, the walls were whitewashed, the wooden columns painted and the altars refurbished.

The first hall holds an image of Tin Hau, together with her guardian generals, and Kwan Tai is honoured in one of the side chapels. The main hall is dedicated to Kun Iam, whose statue occupies an elaborate altar, while the central courtyard contains a porcelain mural of writhing dragons above a stone trough filled with lotus.

The lotus motif and name of the temple date from 1592, when it was built. In those days before land reclamation, it stood on a narrow isthmus connecting China with Macau which the Chinese likened to a lotus flower.

Because the mandarins of Heungshan (Zhongshan) County considered Macau to be part of their territory that had been leased to the Portuguese, they paid regular visits to inspect the mutually-beneficial trade, to mete out justice to Chinese criminals and to remind the Western barbarians that they depended on the favour of the Celestial Empire for their food and water!

Lin Fong Miu was larger than it is today and well able to accommodate the visiting mandarins, and thus it became a favourite stopover. Unfortunately, few Chinese records of these visits have been translated into English, but we do know of one illustrious guest. He was **Commissioner Lin Zexu**, the man who in June 1839 destroyed 20,000 cases of opium in an effort to kill the trade. Three months later Lin visited Macau, where the opium traders spent their summers, and for the first time came face to face with a Western community. (He concluded that the men would not be able to fight because of their close-fitting trousers.) Lin and his entourage stayed at the Lin Fong, which accounts for the statue that was erected here on 3 September 1989, on the 150th anniversary of his visit. One day later, the first shot of what is now known as the Opium War was fired in Kowloon Bay.

The **Hong Kong Miu**, or Temple of the Bazaar, is an excellent example of a thoroughly lived-in, downtown temple, where a visitor will find worshippers from the marketplace. Built in 1860, the temple stands on one side of Largo do Matapau, a square at the end of Rua Cinco de Outubro known for its open-air market with stalls selling bargain clothes, household wares and vegetables.

Before his elevation to a Taoist deity, Hong Kong (no relation to the British territory) was a Han-Dynasty general, renowned for his courage but better known for an unusual rescue. He was fleeing from his enemies when a flock of ducks descended from the sky and obliterated his footprints, facilitating his escape. Out of gratitude, his followers abstain from eating duck on the seventh day of the seventh moon.

The temple has some fine roofs, with porcelain figurines on the ridge-poles, which, unfortunately, are only visible from one of the surrounding modern buildings. The interior consists of prayer halls ranged around a central courtyard. The main hall has an expertly carved altar table with statues of Hong Kong, flanked by Hong Seng, a god of the sea, and Sai San Hau Bong, a military god.

Pou Tai Un on Taipa Island is one of the best-endowed and most picturesque temples in Macau. It was founded in the 19th century by Buddhist monks and the original prayer hall contains images of the Three Precious Buddhas. Since then, both the monastery and temple have been extended and enriched by devotees. There are new pavilions with soaring yellow-tile roofs and an elegant statue of Kun Iam on a marble-columned terrace. The monks live in adjoining buildings. When not busy with prayers, they tend a large vegetable garden and operate a vegetarian restaurant where some of the produce is prepared. Whether vegetarian or not, visitors will enjoy this casual verandah café, where the freshness of the ingredients is matched by the imaginative preparation and wide range of dishes. Beer and soft drinks are available and prices are very low.

The **Temple of the Sleeping Buddha** (Tai Soi Miu) is a very modest example of the famous 'hanging' temples of China, which are built into high cliffs. In Macau, the hill behind St Paul's provides a nearly vertical site, with narrow stairways winding between prayer halls set into the rocks at different levels. The lower halls are devoted to the Taoist God of Justice, goddesses responsible for pregnancy and child care, and the ever-popular Kun Iam. The main hall contains a gilded image of the Buddha reclining with his head resting on one hand. The uppermost shrine houses Chung Kwei, a god of both literature and exorcism. The temple entrance is on Rua da Figueira, a side street between Rua Coelho do Amaral and Rua Tomas Vieira.

The **Lin Kai Miu** (Stream of Mourning Temple) dates from the 17th century, when this area of Patane east of the Camões Grotto was farmland. Today it is a working-class suburb with interesting alleys.

The temple stands in a square off Estrada do Repouso which is usually crowded with hawkers selling cheap clothes and flea-market items. The temple is in need of renovation, so the visitor really feels its age. The main hall is dedicated to Wah Kwong, a god who protects against fire and is also the patron of Cantonese opera troupes. He is shown with a black face and attended by guardian generals. Kun Iam shares a side hall wit Kwan Tai, and another shrine contains an image of the popular Monkey God. For those interested in folk art, this temple has a treat: a collection of 18 clay statuettes of brightly-painted goddesses holding children.

There are many more temples in Macau that merit a brief visit. On Taipa you will want to stop at the **Tin Hau Temple** next to the village bus station. It consists of one splendid hall with a beautifully ornate altar.

壬午冬山王堂張應麟書

名出來

Similarly, no one visiting Coloane village should miss the **Tam Kung Temple**, situated on the waterfront facing China across a narrow channel. Tam Kung is a child-god of seafarers, recognized only in Macau and Hong Kong. Because he is believed to be able to control the weather and protect ships, he is a favourite of fishermen and sailors.

The Tam Kung Temple is small but interesting. It has a fine terracotta roof and an attractive altar. Visitors are invited to admire its two prized possessions: a 1.3 metre (four foot) whalebone carving of a ship carrying images of the Taoist Eight Immortals wearing bowler hats, and the snout of a shark said to have been caught in local waters.

Although Macau seems to have plenty of gods and sufficient temples to house them, the people also need less-exalted deities to attend to their day-to-day problems. This explains the many **neighbourhood shrines** found on pavements, built into apartment blocks or tucked between shop-fronts. Some have a small stone platform with a plaque bearing the name of the god and a bowl for incense, while others are no more than a bristle of burning joss sticks sprouting from a crevice in the pavement. However, all are important for the local residents, who will appeal to the gods for support in a rent dispute or for a repair job by the public works department.

The Imperial Imperative—Fortresses Then and Now

Like other colonial powers, the Portuguese marked their imperial progress by building strongholds to defend each new settlement, to provide necessary shelter and to impress the locals of their intention to stay. The remains of many Portuguese forts can be found along the coasts of Africa, India and Southeast Asia.

Macau, however, was different. In its first 50 years as a Portuguese settlement in the 16th century, it grew rapidly into a rich, international city, with well-armed ships to ward off pirates. The traders and priests saw no need of fortifications, which was a good thing since the Chinese authorities had forbidden them.

The situation changed after the Dutch East India Company was formed in 1602 with the aim of engaging in trade with China. By this time, Holland had the strongest fleet in the world and it usually prevailed over the Portuguese in their encounters. What the Dutch needed was a base of operations and business access to Canton; Macau seemed a logical and easily acquired choice.

The traders in Macau recognized the threat, and in the first 30 years of the 17th century they carried out the construction of a series of forts that would overlook all sea approaches, having convinced the Chinese that they were purely for defence

Rock inscription at A-Ma Temple

against other barbarians and that the traders had no bellicose intentions towards China.

Macau was fortunate in having high ground with commanding views of Praia Grande Bay and what we now call the Inner and Outer harbours. There were a number of sites well suited to the fortress designed by the Marquis of Vauban, a military engineer of genius in the court of Louis XIV.

Vauban recognized that new weaponry made the old castle-style strongholds too vulnerable. Instead, he built his forts in the contours of hills, where they offered minimum exposure to attackers and the greatest field of fire for the defenders. In Macau, the Vauban model is still visible, with walls that slant upwards, bastions at each corner and cannon emplacements in the casements.

The only significant difference is that Macau builders used *chunambo* (or *taipa*) for the walls. This native material, used throughout the Portuguese empire, consists of earth and straw mixed with lime and oyster shells packed tightly in layers between strips of wood. It was believed to be able to withstand cannonballs, but its strength was not tested until the late 19th century when some *chunambo* walls were being demolished. It took a massive 816 kilos (1,800 lbs) of gunpowder to destroy just 130 metres (142 yards) of wall.

The forts and batteries stood atop Monte and Penha hills, on Barra Point at the entrance to the Inner Harbour and at Bomparto and St Francis (which was a battery before the Dutch arrived) to guard Praia Grande Bay. However, they were not finished when they faced their first and fiercest challenge—the 1622 Dutch invasion. (For details, see The Battle of 1622, page 64.)

It was obvious that the forts had been a decisive factor in defeating the invaders, so when **Dom Francisco de Mascarenhas** arrived the following year and became Macau's first full-time governor, he was determined to make Macau impregnable against future attack.

Under his administration, the forts of Monte, Penha, Barra and St Francis were completed and the fort at Guia begun. All were armed with bronze cannon from the local Bocarro foundry, which also supplied the armies of China and Siam. City walls, of an average five metres (16 feet) in height, were built to link the Inner Harbour at Patane to Monte and St Francis, and to connect Bomparto with Penha and the Inner Harbour.

These fortifications doubtless acted as a deterrent, but they were never subject to serious attack, in part because the Dutch, British and other rivals set up their China-trade offices in Macau. Only in the mid-19th century did the Portuguese again feel the need for new defences, this time against the Chinese, whose relations with the city had been badly damaged by the Sino-British Opium Wars.

The mandarins demanded that Macau pull down its walls, but instead the government built new forts on Mong-Ha and Dona Maria hills, both facing the border with China. However, neither was to see action—except when Mong-Ha provided a grandstand for the drama of 25 August 1849, when Mesquita's heroic band slipped across the border and destroyed the fort from which the Chinese were mounting their attack. (See below for details.)

Monte fort, overlooking the ruins of St Paul's, is today a restful retreat, open from dawn to dusk, where the locals practise their *tai chi*, walk their caged birds, prepare their homework or meet friends. The 1835 fire which destroyed most of St Paul's church and the entire college also engulfed the fort. All that remains are the battlements and the old gatehouse, which now houses a café and shop.

The great Bocarro cannon were sold for scrap in the 1870s, but there are some British substitutes to remind visitors of the 1622 battlefield. Four years after that victory, the fort was completed by the Jesuits who provided it with barracks, cisterns and enough stores to weather a two-year siege.

The Jesuits were not to enjoy their new quarters for long. Governor Mascarenhas, who lived in rented rooms in town, asked for an invitation to inspect the fort. He was wined and dined by the priests, who were unaware that he had his soldiers at the gate. After the party, he showed the priests off the premises, which he claimed for himself!

From then until 1746 the fort served as the governor's home and headquarters. During the tenure of Governor Antonio Jose Telles de Menezes, it was also a place best avoided by some government officials. Menezes was a zealous law-and-order reformer. For the lawless he installed a gibbet on the wall of the fort and did not hesitiate to use it.

He also scrutinized those who administered the law and discovered a judge who was behind in his work. Menezes invited the man to dinner. Halfway through, he called in his slaves and had the guest flogged. Then dinner was resumed as if nothing had happened.

The Jesuits returned to their fort after Governor Menezes left, but again not for long. In 1762 they were expelled by order of the Portuguese dictator Pombal and the Monte was abandoned.

Guia fort stands on the highest hill in Macau and offers spectacular views of the entire city, surrounding waters and neighbouring Chinese islands. It is open from dawn to dusk and has a tourist café in one of the old guard-houses. The fort itself was completed in 1638. It occupies an irregular pentagon of about 800 square metres (8,600 square feet). Most of the original barracks and two of the old brickwork turrets remain in good condition.

THE BATTLE OF 1622

Compared with battles fought in contemporary Europe, the action that took place in Macau on 24 June 1622 would be considered no more than a skirmish, although it had many of the dramatic elements of a five-star conflict.

The protagonists were the Portuguese in Macau and the Dutch, who at the beginning of the 17th century were the leading mercantile power in Europe, with the most powerful fleet and the financial support of the Dutch merchants who had grown rich from Portuguese trade in Asia.

With the lure of that trade, the Dutch East India Company was formed in 1602 and soon established outposts in Arabia, India, Siam, southern Japan and Java, with Batavia (present-day Jakarta) from 1618 onwards as its headquarters. In the process, the Dutch often clashed with the Portuguese, but generally, and especially after the loss of Malacca in 1641, won the day—and sometimes a prize cargo of Chinese silks and porcelain as well.

It seemed to Jan Pieterzoon Coen that the time was ripe to capture Macau and take advantage of its access to China. He came to the East in 1619 as governor-general of the Dutch East India Company, and his pet maxim was that 'trade cannot be maintained without war, nor war without trade'. In his opinion, Macau could easily be taken, so he made preparations for an invasion and notified the company's directors in The Hague of his plans.

Their rejection was sent in April 1622, just as the Dutch fleet was leaving Batavia with 13 ships and 1,300 men under the command of Admiral Cornelius Reijersen. Riding the spring monsoon, they came within sight of Macau on 21 June.

Meanwhile on the shore, Lopo Sarmento de Carvalho, Macau's captain-major (acting governor), assessed the situation. Since settling in Macau, the Portuguese had felt no need for defences against the Chinese, who would have objected had they been raised. Only in recent years had Macau recognized the possibility of an attack by Europeans and begun building forts to cover all sea approaches. In 1622, however, none were completed or properly armed. Neither were they properly manned, and Carvalho could muster a scant 50 musketeers. Worse yet, at the time there were only about 100 citizens capable of bearing arms, the rest having gone to Canton to buy silk at the semi-annual fair. So to make up his defence, the captain-major had to rely on the population of slaves, mostly from Africa, and some priests studying at the Jesuit College.

On 23 June the Dutch admiral reconnoitred the coastline and decided to land his troops on Cacilhas Beach (near today's Outer Harbour wharfs). But first he deployed three decoy ships to bombard the São Francisco battery (behind the present site of the Lisboa Hotel), with his sailors shouting that they would capture Macau the following day. The battery responded and managed to knock out one of the ships.

That night the Dutch noisily celebrated their anticipated victory, while on shore Sarmento de Carvalho staged a similar get-together on the fortifications. He also ordered a special rum ration for the slaves the next morning, and doubtless addressed some fervent prayers to St James, the army's patron saint.

The 24th is the feast day of another saint, John the Baptist, but the churches were closed as their congregations prepared for battle. (The Chinese population retreated beyond the border to await the outcome). The Dutch renewed their attack on São Francisco and lost another ship. Then Reijersen and 800 men landed under cover of a smoke screen at Cacilhas Beach.

Cannon emplacement in Monte Fort

They were met by the Macanese musketeers, who fired and struck the admiral, forcing him to return to his ship. The defenders withdrew to the half-finished Monte fort, pursued by the invaders.

In the fort, the cannons were manned by some scholar-priests, including Italian mathematician Jeronomo Rho and the German, Adam Schall von Bell, later the chief astronomer at the court in Peking. Now they put their technical skills to use, firing at the approaching Dutch and hitting their gunpowder wagon. Much of the invaders' ammunition was destroyed, along with their morale. The Dutch captain turned towards Guia Hill in the hope of gaining higher ground. Instead his troops came under fire from Macanese and Negro snipers, so he decided to retreat. Carvalho saw what was happening and rallied his rag-tag army with the shout: 'St James and at them!'

The defenders became attackers, storming down Monte Hill and slaughtering every Dutchman in sight. The slaves proved the most effective fighters. Inspired by a combination of rum and loyalty, they gave no quarter, beheading some of the enemy—in honour, some said, of St John the Baptist. One Negress, dressed as a man, wielded an axe with devastating effect, much to the admiration of the Portuguese soldiers.

The Dutch survivors scrambled back to their boats, while on the battlefield the slaves were given their freedom. In St Paul's, the victorious priests gave thanks with a Te Deum Laudamus.

The defenders had lost six citizens, some slaves and much property, against 300 Dutch dead. The battle had lasted only two hours, but it helped to keep Macau under Portuguese rule for the next 350 years.

Dominating the fort is the graceful **lighthouse**. Built in 1865 and the oldest on the China coast, its beam can be seen for 32 kilometres (20 miles) on a clear night. Until it was electrified in 1909 it was powered by paraffin lamps, one of which is on display in the Maritime Museum. You need permission from the Marine Department to go inside the lighthouse.

Next to the lighthouse stands the **Chapel of Our Lady of Guia**. It has a simple façade of whitewashed stone with cream trim around the pediment and entrance. Inside there is an attractive altar, some old paintings and a gravestone with a worn inscription which states mysteriously that the remains interred beneath 'do not deserve such an honourable sepulchre'.

The Guia fort might not have witnessed enemy fire, but it has suffered plenty of nature's fury. In fact, before the days of radio, Macau residents relied on signals raised above the fort to indicate the proximity, direction and wind speed of the typhoons which roar in every summer and autumn from the Pacific Ocean.

Those signals are still hoisted, and when not in use are stored in the gatehouse of the fort. Made of black metal mesh, they spell out a series of warnings. For instance, an inverted three-dimentional 'T' is the Number Three signal that means winds of 22–33 knots are expected. The pyramid-shaped Number Eight signal means the storm is very close (and all ferry services have stopped), while the Number Ten signal, in the form of a cross, indicates that the typhoon has arrived.

The fortress of St James of the Bar (São Tiago da Barra), **Barra fort**, is a leading tourist attraction and award-winning example of heritage conservation, consisting of a Portuguese inn built into the foundations of a 17th-century fort.

This new-found fame is quite appropriate, since the fort was a well-known landmark for most of its working life. Like similar fortifications in Macau, it was incomplete when the Dutch invaded in 1624, but was imposing enough to deter them from entering the Inner Harbour. In those days, the entrance channel was much narrower, and the fort's fire-power had sufficient range to cover the sand-barred passage.

When construction was completed in 1629, it looked like a small fortified town. The *chunambo* walls, set in stone foundations, rose more than nine metres (30 feet) out of the sea. They were almost six metres (19 feet) thick at the base and tapered to 3.5 metres (11 feet) at the top.

The main platform occupied 4,807 square metres (51,750 square feet) and supported a dozen 24-pound cannon, four 50-pounders, a cistern with a capacity of 3,000 tonnes of water and quarters for a commander and 60 men. On the hill above was a guard-house and six 24-pound cannon. In the basement were stores for supplies and ammunition.

In 1740, a chapel was installed and dedicated to St James (São Tiago), patron saint of the army. His statue, uniformed and brandishing a sword, occupied the altar—at least when the soldiers were watching! According to legend, St James would patrol the fort at night and there would be mud on his boots the next morning. Cleaning them was the special duty of one of the guards, and it was reported that if he was negligent the saint would strike him a blow on the head.

The fort continued to be garrisoned although it was never attacked. Nevertheless, it played a part in a modern conflict. During the Second World War, Macau, as Portuguese territory, was neutral and offered refuge to tens of thousands of Portuguese, Chinese, White Russians and others fleeing from Hong Kong and China. The city was blockaded and food was scarce, so the captain of Barra fort bartered the last of his artillery for rice.

After the war, parts of the fort were pulled down to make way for a road and new houses. What remained was taken over briefly by the marine police, but was deemed unsafe. It was closed and apparently doomed to demolition.

Instead, the government came up with an imaginative scheme—to create a traditional inn, or *pousada*, within the historic site. The task was given to the former Department of Tourism and local architect Nuno Jorge was put in charge of the project, called **Pousada de São Tiago**.

Jorge faced unprecedented problems and invented solutions as he went along. For instance, rather than tear down the old banyan trees that had grown into the old platform, he incorporated them into the design. This meant matching the contours of the buildings with the canopies of the branches, and restoring the foundations without damaging the roots.

The original entrance was reconstructed, complete with a water trough bearing the date 1629. When workers found water from underground springs seeping through the major structural walls, instead of plugging the springs, the architect made it part of the decor. Water from the springs now glistens on the fern-clad lobby wall and ripples down tiled channels on either side of the entrance stairway.

The old water cistern was also found to be in working order, so Jorge converted it to a European-style fountain that plays for guests on the café terrace. The chapel was totally restored and is a popular venue for weddings and marital reconfirmations.

The basic model for the *pousada* was a stately colonial home of the 18th century. Craftsmen in Lisbon supplied wood and leather furniture, crystal lamps, curtains and furnishings to the exact specifications. Then, to give the building a true sense of place, terracotta tile floors and tubular roof tiles were ordered from China—likewise the 'typically Portuguese' blue-and-white tile pictures found throughout the *pousada*.

The work took four years and far exceeded the budget, but the result, now privately owned, is a priceless heirloom for Macau and an essential sight for every visitor, whether staying in one of the marvellous guest rooms or enjoying a meal or drink in the incomparable setting.

At the other end of town, the **Fortress of Mong-Ha** is also devoted to tourism, but behind the scenes, because this is where the Tourism School is located. There is a *pousada* here as well as a workaday hotel used mainly by official visitors and government servants waiting to move into their own quarters. All visitors, however, are welcome in the restaurant.

Those who built and garrisoned Mong-Ha would find this devotion to hospitality difficult to comprehend. For them, the fort was a symbol of a beleaguered city in one of its darkest hours. The fort stands on a hill overlooking the border with China. During the Ming Dynasty, it had been known as Lotus Hill to the Chinese, but by the mid-19th century it represented an unwelcome European presence.

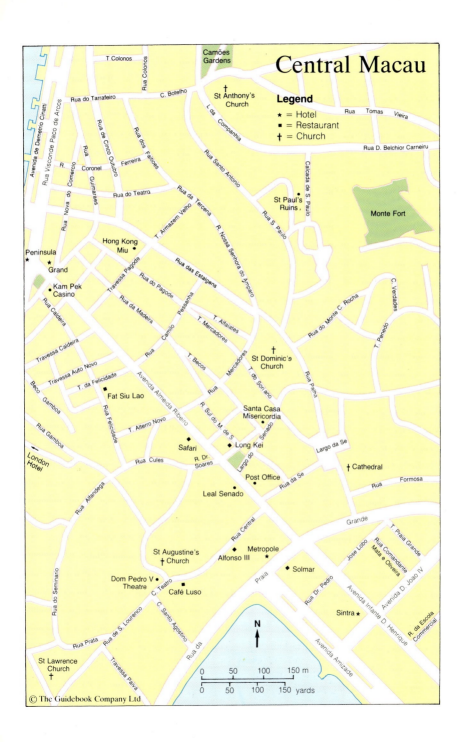

Explorers and Adventurers

The late-18th century was a busy time for travellers around the Pacific. They included explorers and adventurers, artists and scientists, missionaries and merchants. Most came from Europe, and Macau was a welcome port of call thanks to its strategic location and famous hospitality.

Not everyone enjoyed their stay. In 1769 the British traveller William Hickey spent a few hours in the city, which he declared 'bespoke the acme of poverty and misery'. The Portuguese Bishop Alexander Guimaraes had longer to consider an opinion and later complained of rowdy festivals, betel-nut chewing in church, gambling, women drinking alcohol and bearded priests.

Others were more appreciative of Macau. In December 1779, the *Discovery* and the *Resolution* dropped anchor in Praia Bay. They had carried Captain James Cook and his men on some incredible voyages of discovery all over the Pacific, and in the previous year had tried but failed to find a northwest passage to the Atlantic. In the process, Cook had nevertheless mapped the coast of Alaska and confirmed the existence of the Bering Strait. Then he sailed south to the Hawaiian islands, where he was killed in a local skirmish.

The ships' officers tried without enthusiasm or success to continue the explorations. Finally they decided to head for home and stopped en route in Macau to provision the ships and sell a cargo of furs to the Chinese for 2,000 pounds sterling. The Macanese offered the men bed, board, entertainment and sympathy for the loss of their leader. One of the officers was John Webber, an artist, who recorded the visit in some fine engravings of Macau scenes.

Eight years later another explorer arrived. He was Jean Francois de Galaup, Count La Perouse, who had been sent by the French government to outdo the British by finding the northwest passage that had eluded Cook. With his frigates *La Boussole* and *L'Astrolabe*, the Frenchman followed in the wake of the English explorer—with the same lack of success.

Instead the Count turned his attention to China and to its gateway, Macau. Here he set up a small observatory on a hill in the Camões Gardens, and trained his telescopes and sextants on the mysterious empire that was closed to all but a few Westerners. Since there was at the time a flourishing

French community in the city he was the celebrity of the season and his observatory became a local attraction.

In August 1787 La Perouse set sail again for the northwest, where he discovered the strait between Hokkaido and Sakhalin which today bears his name. Then he headed south and reached Australia where he identified what is now La Perouse Point. His last message was sent from Australia in January 1788 and his fate remained a mystery until the wreck of *L'Astrolabe* was discovered 38 years later on Vanikoro in the Solomon Islands.

Such visitors were treated with respect and warmth by Macau, but there was one arrival who achieved a different kind of fame within days of coming ashore. This was Count Maritus Benyovsky, the leader of a sick and starving group who arrived in a rickety boat on 22 September 1771.

The Macanese were fascinated by the new arrivals—especially when one in female clothing was discovered to be a man—and gave them a welcome that proved too lavish. As the Count recorded in his diary, 'For the first days my companies lodged in a public house and the excess and avidity with which they devoured the bread and fresh provisions which they were supplied with, cost thirteen of them their lives.'

The Count's story was now revealed. He had been born, the son of a cavalry general on the Hungarian-Polish border, in 1741. He had become a military officer and fought with the Poles against the Russians, who captured him and his company in 1769. They were sent to Kamchatka in Siberia, where Benyovsky became tutor to the Russian governor's daughters, one of whom, Afanasia, fell in love with him. In 1771 the Count and his men escaped after a fight in which the governor was killed. Afanasia insisted on leaving with them and, dressed as a boy and calling herself Achilles, helped them seize a boat. They sailed to California where they took on a cargo of furs, then headed back to Japan. They were turned away and drifted down the coast to Macau.

Unfortunately for Afanasia, Benyovsky was married and did not share her passion. According to the Macanese, who were partial to love stories with unhappy endings, she died of a broken heart in Macau that winter. The Count departed in February 1772 for France, where he persuaded the court to help him establish a colony in Madagascar. With financial help from a company in Maryland, he attempted to establish himself as king and in 1786 was killed by a French expeditionary force. The story of Afanasia and her dashing Count, however, lived on in Macau.

Macau maintained good relations with China for almost three centuries. Both Portugal and China benefited from the status of the territory, and both understood that the mandarins could win any dispute by halting food supplies. The situation deteriorated in the 18th century as merchants from Britain, America and Europe took over the China trade with the import of opium. This led to the 1840 Opium War and the cession of Hong Kong to Britain.

Macau suffered from the Chinese defeat. Its rich foreign residents moved to the new colony, and the mandarins—powerless against the British—saw an opportunity to avenge their loss of face by attacking the vulnerable Portuguese.

In 1846 a new governor arrived in Macau. He was **João Ferreira do Amaral**, a naval hero who had lost his right arm in battle and an authoritarian patriot determined to strengthen the city's defences and brook no compromise with the Chinese. He laid the foundations for the Mong-Ha fort and another on nearby Dona Maria hill.

The Chinese objected, calling this an act of war. Many senators also opposed the governor's policy, preferring the traditional pragmatic approach to the mandarins. Amaral refused to back down, even after several attempts on his life. Someone tried to poison his food, and a venomous snake was placed in his bed.

Finally, in August 1849 when he was out riding near the border, he was ambushed by a group of Chinese who dragged him from his horse and stabbed him to death. They then cut off his head and left hand, and took them in triumph to Canton.

Macau reacted with panic. Chinese residents retreated to China as the mandarins moved men and ammunition into the fort of Pakshanlan, 1.5 kilometres (one mile) north of the border. The senate conferred with the army council, but everyone agreed that the situation was hopeless. Everyone, that is, except a young Macanese lieutenant named **Vicente Nicolau de Mesquita**, the council's aide-de-camp.

He proposed to storm the fort with a band of 36 volunteers. The command agreed, and on the morning of 25 August a force of 120 Portuguese soldiers stood guard on the Macau side of the border, within sight of a Chinese army 2,000 strong, 500 of whom were on duty in Pakshanlan. They maintained a steady bombardment as Mesquita and his men crept across the border and approached the fort. By the time the Chinese saw them it was too late.

The Macanese were close enough to the fort to render its artillery useless and within minutes they had captured the stronghold and killed those defenders who had not fled. Mesquita spiked the guns, blew up the powder magazine and raised a Portuguese flag. Hearing the explosions, the people of Macau waited in trepidation, fearing the worst. When they received news of the victory, they made their way to Mong-Ha to cheer Mesquita and his heroic band.

In honour of the event, a new **border gate** was built and inscribed with the date August 1849. Construction of the Mong-Ha fort was briefly resumed, but it was not until 1864 that work began in earnest by order of the new governor, Coelho do Amaral. Although sharing the same name, he was the exact opposite of his murdered predecessor and was responsible for building the Praia Grande seawall, planting banyan trees and providing Macau with such amenities as street lighting and a sewage system.

Mong-Ha was completed in 1866. It had an area of 650 square metres (7,000 square feet) and consisted of an ammunition store, an observatory and platforms mounted with two quick-firing 65-millimetre Armstrong guns. Inside the fort were the soldiers' quarters and stores, linked by narrow stairways. The only entrance was through a massive wooden door with strap-hinges and cast-iron locks.

Built of heavy masonry and reinforced concrete, the fort was considered impregnable, but was never tested. The Chinese threat receded with the shift of trade and hostility to Hong Kong and the new treaty ports on the China coast. The buildings were gradually abandoned and in the 1970s the military moved out.

The idea of converting some of the old barracks into a tourism school was inspired by the rehabilitation of the Pousada de São Tiago, and in 1982 the first trainees began six-month courses in hotel work. Since then, the school has expanded to cover many aspects of the tourist industry. The Mong-Ha *pousada* was initially used for the students' practical training and for tourist promotions. Later it was decided to make it a working inn. The rest of the fort is open for inspection. You can pass through the entrance and clamber up the stairs to the platform, which offers some excellent views, though none of the border which is now hidden behind tall factory and apartment blocks.

The **fort of St Francis** (São Francisco) is the only monument in Macau that has been rebuilt as a fort. Today its handsome pink and white stone buildings are overshadowed by the Lisboa Hotel (where the A Galera restaurant features it as a view!), but it once stood proudly on a small protruding point on the north shore of Praia Grande Bay.

The original fort played a critical role in the victory over the Dutch in 1622 and, when completed seven years later, was a key bastion of defence, linked as it was by the city wall to Monte and the Inner Harbour. The fortress contained a monastery founded by Spanish Franciscan monks from the Philippines in 1580, and among its armaments was a culverin capable of firing 35-pound iron shot a distance of 2.5 kilometres (1.5 miles).

The original fort (formerly a battery) and monastery were demolished to make way for the present buildings in 1864, which were used as military barracks until a few years ago when the security forces took over. It has a collection of vintage armoured cars and other historical items, but unfortunately it is not open to the public.

No other forts in Macau have survived except as the foundations for something

Vignette

Um governo sem mando, um bispo tal,
De freiras virtuosas um covil,
Três conventos de frades, cinco mil
Nhon's e chinas cristãos, que obram mui mal.
Uma Sé que hoje existe tal e qual,
Catorze prebendados sem ceitil
Muita pobreza, muita mulher vil,
Cem portugeses, tudo em un curral;
Seis fortes, cem soldados, um tambor,
Três frequesias, cujo ornato é pau,
Um Vigário-Geral, sem promotor,
Dois colégios, e um deles muito mau,
Um senado que a tudo é superior,
É quanto Portugal tem em Macau.

A Governor without power, likewise a Bishop,
A covy of virtuous monks,
Three convents of friars, five thousand
Mestizos and Chinese Christians, who work very badly.
A Cathedral that survives more or less,
Fourteen stipendaries without stipends,
Many poor, many vile women,
A hundred Portuguese, all corralled together;
Six forts, a hundred soldiers, one drum,
Three parish churches simply adorned,
A Vicar-General without hopes of promotion,
Two colleges, one of them a disgrace,
A senate that is all powerful,
This is Portugal in Macau.

Manuel Barbosa du Bocage (1790)
Translated by Shann Davies

else. The Bomparto walls line the street of the same name that leads up to the Bela Vista Hotel, itself built into the ruins of the old Bomparto fort. The present security forces' building on Taipa Island also stands on the foundations of a fort. However, no trace of Penha fort is visible around the Bishop's Palace that now occupies the site, while Dona Maria is now just a pleasant belvedere—and a famous bend on the Grand Prix circuit.

City of the Name of God - Churches and Charities

When Pope Alexander VI signed the 1494 Treaty of Tordesillas that split the world for missionary purposes among Portugal, Spain and several other nations, none of the parties knew where the line would pass through Asia. In the next century, representatives of both countries arrived on the scene to find that Portugal's patrimony included China, Japan and the Indies, while Spain could only claim the Philippines.

This did not deter the Spaniards from attempting to evangelize the great pagan masses of China and Japan. However, the key battles for Asian souls that were fought from the 16th to the 19th century involved Catholic orders at first and later Protestant sects, rather than nations. Macau, as the gateway to China and the educational hub of the Jesuit mission, played a role in many of these conflicts. In the earliest days, it also experienced a church-building boom.

The churches built in the late 16th century were simple structures, usually made of bamboo and rush matting, and were regularly destroyed by fire and storm. Only when enough money became available were larger and more durable buildings constructed in *chunambo* and stone. These were replaced in the 18th and early-19th centuries with churches in the distinctive neo-baroque style favoured by the colonial Portuguese and Spaniards. The new buildings were made of stone and faced with pastel-washed plaster. Typically they had flat wooden ceilings and altars that verged on the rococo, with Romanesque statues, neo-classical columns, candelabra and stucco decorations.

The fact that these churches have been regularly renovated and occasionally rebuilt bears witness to the tenacity of faith among the people of Macau. There is a morning mass every day in virtually all the churches to serve the territory's 23,500 adherents of the Catholic faith, who also observe a profusion of saints' days and religious festivals.

St Paul's (São Paulo), the most popular emblem of Macau, is a free-standing ruin that dramatizes the spirit of the city. This is fitting for a church that was acclaimed second in grandeur only to St Peter's in Rome. St Paul's was founded by the Jesuits at

the same time as their **college**, where Ricci, Schall Von Bell and other missionaries prepared for service in China.

When the original wooden building burnt down in 1601, it was replaced by a new stone and *chunambo* church modelled after the Jesuit church in Rome. St Paul's opened on Christmas Eve 1603, with a congregation of 300 Portuguese. What they saw was described by the English trader Peter Mundy in 1637: 'The roof is of the fairest arch that yet I ever saw...carved in wood, curiously gilt and painted with exquisite colours, as vermillion azure, etc.'

The church was very spacious (as suggested by the site today): 19 metres (63 feet) wide, 36.5 metres (120 feet) long and 11 metres (37 feet) high. There were three naves, three chapels and two altars. Eight wooden pillars supported the roof, and the chapel walls were lined with fine Japanese wood.

The church contained many treasures, including reliquaries with an arm bone of **St Francis Xavier** and relics of Christians martyred in Japan and Indochina, along with religious paintings by European and Japanese artists. The latter are now housed in the St Francis Xavier chapel on Coloane and in St Joseph's Seminary.

The stone façade dates from the 1620s, when Japanese and Chinese Christian masons worked under the supervision of an Italian Jesuit. It cost 30,000 taels of silver, paid by the government, and was instantly recognized as a prime example of a 'sermon in stone', where different cultures mingled in one faith.

The church flourished until 1762 when the Jesuits were expelled. The Bishopric (traditionally anti-Jesuit) became responsible for St Paul's, while the government took over the college and put it to various non-scholastic uses. In 1831 the prince regent's battalion was billetted here, and four years later tragedy struck when a fire started in the woodshed and quickly engulfed the entire Jesuit complex. The college was totally destroyed, together with much of the fort and most of the church.

Since then, the surviving façade has been studied, admired and written about by generations of visitors. Sir John Bowring, governor of Hong Kong from 1854 to 1859, featured it in a hymn:

> *In the Cross of Christ I glory,*
> *Towering o'er the wrecks of time;*
> *All the light of sacred story*
> *Gathers round its head sublime.*

Although the stone carvings are cleaned regularly, it is difficult to appreciate them fully from below. The uppermost tier is in the form of a cross-crowned pediment bearing a bronze dove (cast by Bocarro) surrounded by stars, the sun and the moon. On the tier below stands a statue of Christ in a niche decorated with fleur-delys and chrysanthemums — the Japanese national flower that was incorporated in the design by the exiled Christian Japanese. On either side are angels with the cross and scourging pillar, obelisks carved with the names of St Peter and St Paul, and smiling lions, the Chinese symbol for strength and courage.

The third tier is the most elaborate. A statue of the Virgin occupies the middle niche, along with six angels playing musical instruments or praying. On the panel to the right is a seven-headed monster under a praying Virgin, captioned in Chinese, 'The Holy Mother tramples the dragon's head'. Beside it is a carving of a skeleton with an arrow piercing its side and the message, 'Remember death and thou shalt never sin'.

The left-hand panels feature a Portuguese sailing ship and a fallen devil pierced by an arrow that is captioned 'It was the Devil's temptation that made man sinful'.

The second tier contains three archways and Bocarro's bronze statues of four Jesuit saints: Ignatius Loyola, Francis Xavier, Francis Borgia and Aloysius Gonzaga.

St Dominic's (São Domingos) is one of the most attractive churches in Macau, with probably the bloodiest past. It stands in the heart of the town, a block from Leal Senado Square, with its beautifully balanced façade of cream-washed stone embellished with white stucco moulding, Ionic columns and stone urns. The windows are shuttered with green louvres and the doors are made of teak and oak.

Inside is a superb baroque altar containing statues of the Virgin and Child and two saints. Above is an ornate pediment and below, a thicket of candles and vases. The side altars contain some exquisite statues of saints, with their heads and hands carved in ivory by local artists. The nave is divided into three aisles by cream and white pillars supporting delicately moulded arches and a wooden ceiling of pale turquoise panels.

The whole atmosphere could not be more tranquil, but in its time St Dominic's was a battleground. The original church with an adjoining monastery was founded by Dominican friars in the 1590s. It flourished and one of the order became the bishop of Macau. After ten years, however, he was recalled following disputes with the senate.

This seemed to doom the church to conflict. In 1642, after the city had celebrated the restoration of the Portuguese crown, there was fighting in the streets because the governor had reneged on a promise to free some imprisoned Spaniards. In the struggle between the governor's troops and those of the senate, a man sought refuge in St Dominic's where mass was being celebrated. The mob pursued him inside and stabbed him to death in front of the high altar.

Macau's most significant civil strife took place at the beginning of the 18th century and revolved around the **Rites Controversy** which split the Catholic church and fatally damaged its work in China. In the spirit of Matteo Ricci, Schall Von Bell and

Verbiest, who had become members of China's intellectual elite, the Jesuits accepted Chinese ancestor worship as a secular rite rather than a religious observance. The monastic orders, on the other hand, condemned the practice as a heresy which the Chinese had to disavow before being confirmed Christians. Not suprisingly, the Jesuits made far more converts, in particular among the mandarins and literati.

The Vatican eventually ruled in favour of the friars in 1705, when Pope Clement XI sent a legate, **Charles de Tournon**, to deliver his decree to China. In Peking he was received politely, but Emperor Kangxi remarked that people incapable of understanding Confucianism had to be small-minded.

In 1707 de Tournon arrived in Macau to promulgate the decree. Opinion was strongly divided among the citizens, but Bishop Casal sided with the Jesuits and refused the legate's demand, with orders for the churches of Macau to do likewise. In response, the Dominicans and Augustinians shifted their support to de Tournon and posted his notices outside their churches. The governor sent troops to tear them down, so provoking the Dominican friars that they locked themselves in their church and pelted the soldiers with stones.

The battle ended when the troops broke in and arrested some friars, who spent several days in the dungeons of Monte fort. De Tournon was placed under house arrest and died in 1710. The Jesuits in China were gradually forced to accept the papal decree, which remained in force until 1939.

In 1834 anti-clerical sentiment in Portugal prompted the government to close all monasteries and forbid religious orders to own property. As a result, the Dominicans in Macau had to sell their 24 houses, 66 shops and various tracts of land. Their monastery was taken over by the government and used variously as a barracks, stable, fire brigade and telephone exchange before being demolished to make way for Rua da Palha and Travessa dos Algibebes.

The other church involved in the Rites Controversy was **St Augustine's** (Santo Agostinho), which stands on a hill behind the praia and Leal Senado, where it shares a square that could have been transplanted from Portugal with the Dom Pedro V Theatre, St Joseph's Seminary and Casa Ricci.

St Augustine's has a simple façade, cream-coloured with white stucco trim, a pediment containing a statue of the Madonna and Child, and a neo-Grecian portico. The door is usually open and visitors can explore the spacious triple-aisled nave and the altar area. Here the dominant feature is a statue of **Christ bearing the cross**. This is the centrepiece of the Passos procession on the first day of Lent. (See Festivals of East and West, page 39.)

An early Macanese legend explains how the *passos* or 'steps' brought the statue here. Soon after the original church was built on this site in 1586, the image washed up on the shore and insisted on being taken to St Augustine's, but the local authorities disapproved and transferred it to the cathedral. Mysteriously the statue vanished, only to appear in the Augustinian church. The authorities tried to transfer it again and again, but failing each time they finally allowed it to remain in its chosen place. The statue also features in a Chinese legend. As a consequence of the Rites Controversy, the Augustinian friars were deported from Macau in 1711, only to return in 1712. That same year there was a desperate food shortage. This was probably due to China holding back supplies, but the locals attributed it to the cancellation of the Passos, and demanded that 'the man with the cross on his shoulders' walk the streets again. They even offered to pay the expenses. The bishop agreed, and of course the famine ended!

In front of the altar are several worn tombstones. Some mark the remains of Augustinian missionaries, such as Alvaro de Benavente, vicar apostolic of Jiangxi Province. Another tomb once held the remains of Charles de Tournon, who died in the monastery then attached to the church. (He was finally interred in Rome).

Although the Rites Controversy occupied Macau's attention, it was a minor diversion compared with the great romance of the time. This began in 1706 with the arrival of the captain of marines, Antonio de Albuquerque Coelho, a dashing young man in search of a career and a wife. For the latter he chose Maria de Moura, the wealthiest orphan in Macau, who had many suitors, including Lieutenant Henrique de Noronha—even though she was only nine years old.

Antonio won her heart and in 1709 the two were betrothed, with Maria legally sequestered away from his rivals. But Dom Henrique did not give up, and made several attempts on Albuquerque's life. He failed, but wounded the captain in the arm. Gangrene set in, and when Antonio learned that it had to be amputated, he offered to free Maria from her vow. She responded like a true heroine: she would marry him just as long as he was alive, even if his two legs were cut off.

The couple were wedded in 1710—and escaped a further assault when another jealous suitor sent his assassins to the wrong church. They lived happily together for four years. When Maria gave birth to a son, Antonio prepared a grand celebration, but it all came to a sudden tragic end when Maria and the baby died.

Albuquerque later became a successful governor in Macau and Timor, but his most famous legacy is the epitaph he had inscribed on a plaque beside the altar of St Augustin's: 'In this urn are the bones of the bodies of Maria de Moura de Vasconcellos and her daughter Dona Ignes and of the right arm of her husband Antonio D'Albuquerque.'

Maria was also long remembered by a popular song with the rather odd lyrics, 'She is not so beautiful, nor yet so good-looking that, if not for her money, why should Maria cause such a commotion?' Antonio never remarried.

São Domingos Church

The **Cathedral** (Largo da Sé), restored in 1938, occupies its own square at the top of the steps leading from the main street. Though its neo-gothic towers and massive nave are of little architectural interest, it is worth a visit for its fine stained-glass windows. It is also the focus of attention at Easter as the first stage of the Passos procession. The first cathedral in Macau, the Church of Our Lady (later the Church of St Lazarus), was constructed of wood on this site in 1576 and declared to be the mother church of the vast Macau diocese, which then included China, Japan and the adjacent islands. This was later replaced with a building of *chunambo* in 1623, built on the cathedral's present location, which survived until 1850 when it was reconstructed in stone under the supervision of the Macanese architect, Tomos de Aquino, and consecrated by the bishop, D Jeronimo J de Matta. The new cathedral was extensively damaged in the 1874 typhoon and remained under constant repair. In 1938 it was restored by D Jose da Costa Nunes and renovated in the 1980s.

After many years, the church of **St Joseph** (São Jose) is again open to visitors. It is part of the rambling old seminary founded by the Jesuits in 1728 to train Chinese priests. After the expulsion of the Jesuits, the seminary was run by the French Lazarists until the Society of Jesus returned. St Joseph's ceased to be a working seminary in 1966 when the seminarians turned tail as a result of the Cultural Revolution in China.

The church, built between 1746 and 1758, is one of the most delightful places in Macau. It is quite small and perfectly proportioned, with a domed roof and three baroque altars framed by slender turned columns where some fine statuary is displayed. The church has outstanding acoustics.

As befits a church in the Iberian style, there is a cloistered garden adjoining it. There is an old-fashioned well in the middle, surrounded by well-kept flower beds and shrubs, all set off by the weathered walls of the seminary with their narrow windows covered by faded green wooden louvres.

The seminary has many treasures, including paintings by Japanese Christian exiles who lived and worked in Macau in the early 17th century. There is also an extensive library of religious books and furniture salvaged from St Paul's. Unfortunately, the seminary floors cannot withstand an unlimited number of visitors. If and when funds become available for restoration work, the treasures will be put on display. Until then you will need to meet Father Teixeira, Macau's resident historian and patriarch, who lives in the seminary. He delights in sharing his wealth of knowledge and enthusiasm with interested visitors. The church and garden are open from 10 am–4 pm daily except Wednesdays.

The impressive church of **St Lawrence** (São Laurenço) stands in twin-towered majesty on Rua de São Laurenço, above the Government Palace and Praia Grande

Bay. It is Macau's most fashionable church, as can be seen before and after mass when parishioners pause for conversation on the elegant double staircase and around the spacious, palm-shaded courtyard.

Visitors should go in to admire the splendid nave, with its magnificent wooden ceiling painted turquoise, white and gold beams, and fine chandeliers. The high altar contains a statue of St Lawrence as a handsome young man dressed in gorgeous robes. Above him is a cherub holding a crown and, behind him, a stained-glass window featuring a dove of peace. A wooden lamb hangs over them all.

In recent years the organizers of the Macau Music Festival have recognized the dramatic setting and acoustic possibilities of St Lawrence's, and hold scheduled choral concerts here. The church is open from 10 am–4 pm daily.

The **chapel of St Francis Xavier** is a regular pilgrimage destination for Japanese and Catholic visitors, who make their way to Coloane Island and the simple baroque-style chapel that stands next to the village in a garden which also contains a memorial celebrating a local victory over pirates in 1910.

There is nothing simple about the interior. Its most precious treasure is a bone from the arm of St Francis, who died in 1522 on Shang Chuan, an island 83 kilometres (50 miles) away. This relic was en route to Japan in 1619 when word was received of new anti-Christian persecution there. Nonetheless, it remained in Japan until 1633 or 1634 when it was brought to Macau and kept in St Paul's until the fire. Afterwards it was moved to St Anthony's church and then to the Cathedral before finally ending up in St Joseph's.

The chapel was built in 1928, but not until 50 years later was the relic, in an ornate silver reliquary, brought here—in a procession led by a jazz band playing 'When the Saints Go Marching In'. Today it occupies a special altarpiece, which often provides a backdrop for services for Japanese couples who come here to confirm their marriages. Some are Christian, some Buddhist, but all revere the saint who brought the Word and other Western ideas to Japan in the 16th century.

Among the many other sacred bones in the chapel, some belong to Japanese martyred in the late-16th and early-17th centuries. Other bones were brought from Indochina and include those of the first Christian martyrs of Vietnam from the 17th century. The resident priest delights in showing off the treasures.

A chapel of a very different kind is found on the other side of Coloane. **Our Lady of Sorrows** was built in 1966 to serve the members of the leper colony of Ka Ho who live here in peaceful isolation, attended by Catholic priests. Now cured, some of them remain here with their families. The church is contemporary in design and features a great bronze crucifix over the door and a charming grotto containing a statue of the Virgin.

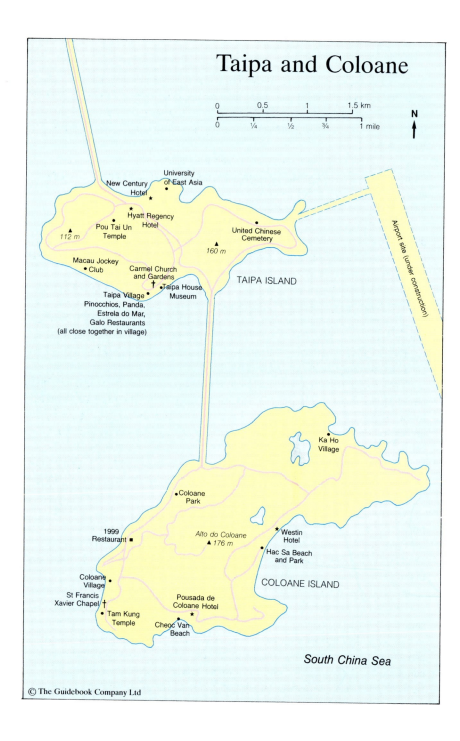

The chapel dedicated to **Our Lady of Penha** is now open to the public. It is part of the Bishop's Palace on top of Penha Hill, long renowned for its breathtaking views. The first chapel was founded in 1622 by sailors in an expression of gratitude for having escaped capture by the Dutch. The present chapel, built in 1935, is open from 10 am–4 pm daily.

Other churches in Macau include **St Anthony's** (Santo Antonio), near the Camões Gardens and the Old Protestant Cemetery. The original church, founded around 1558, was the earliest in Macau. It was destroyed and rebuilt many times, most recently in 1930, and contains little of interest to the tourist.

St Lazarus (São Lazaro), off Rua do Campo in the heart of the restored Lazaro district, is another modern building that is open for daily and Sunday mass. It stands on the site of Our Lady of Hope Hermitage, established outside the old city walls as a refuge for lepers.

The church of **Our Lady of Carmel** commands a beautiful site on the small hill between Taipa village and the old Taipa praia. It is only a century old and well-maintained. It has an attractive neo-Gothic nave and a classic altar, but is usually closed. The gardens in front are well worth a visit. (See Gardens and Grottoes, page 98.)

The chapels of **Our Lady of Guia** and **St James** are included in descriptions of the Guia and São Tiago da Barra fortresses. (See pages 66 and 67.)

Along with their faith, the Portuguese brought charity to Macau, where the Catholic church, rather than the social services department of the government, continues to shoulder much of the responsibility for sheltering the homeless, feeding the hungry, ministering to the impoverished sick and educating disadvantaged and handicapped children.

This admirable tradition is spearheaded by the **Holy House of Mercy** (Santa Casa da Misericordia), with headquarters located in the stately white-stone, double-arcaded building in Leal Senado Square.

The Santa Casa was founded by Queen Leonor of Portugal in 1498, with the principal aim of caring for women and children widowed and orphaned as a result of the Portuguese explorations. An office of the charity was established in Macau in 1568 by Dom Belchior Carneiro. Throughout the centuries its president was the head of the Leal Senado.

In the golden days of the Japan–China Voyage, the Santa Casa—like everyone else in Macau—invested heavily in the cargoes, sometimes earning huge profits, sometimes losing everything.

The charity's fortunes declined with those of Macau, but fortunately one of the Santa Casa's heaviest burdens—large numbers of orphan girls who were taken in, educated and, if not sought in marriage, usually placed in domestic service or assigned to a convent—sometimes provided new funds when they were most needed.

A few orphans, however, more than repaid their benefactor. The best-known was **Marta Merop**, a Chinese foundling (all races and creeds were accepted) who left the Santa Casa and lived with (and possibly married) a British trader. She was a very intelligent girl who learned languages and business quickly. When the trader had to return home, she formed her own company and operated her own ships, becoming possibly the wealthiest woman on the China coast. Before she died in 1829 she was married to the church and left all her money to the Holy House. (She is the heroine of Austin Coates' novel, *City of Broken Promises.*)

The charity no longer runs an orphanage, but it does have a home for the aged, a soup kitchen, several clinics and the leprosaurium on Coloane Island.

The upper floor of the headquarters can be visited during office hours. Enter through the door on the left side of the building. A spacious reception hall opens onto the balcony and is hung with portraits of Marta Merop and other benefactors. A glass case under a picture of Bishop Carneiro contains his rosary and skull.

The Santa Casa is not the only charity in Macau. Other Christian organisations operate free schools and hospitals, sheltered workshops, subsidized housing and even a hospice.

The Colonial Presence—Stately Homes and Offices

One of the delights of visiting Macau is to stroll along a street or lane and suddenly find a building transposed from another time and place. These surprises could be newly-renovated mansions that have long served as government offices, or private homes half-hidden behind garden walls and rampant foliage.

Some buildings are excellent examples of baroque and neo-classical architecture, but most are colonial hybrids—China-coast adaptations of European models. The predominant style is Iberian, but there are many reminders that the British paid the rent on many houses here. They are reassuring souvenirs of a leisurely past that survives in part because they continue to be useful.

The majority of these buildings date from the 19th century with a few from the late-18th and early-20th centuries. They were commissioned by merchants, priests and administrators, but with few exceptions their architects are now unknown.

By general consensus, the **Loyal Senate** (Leal Senado) is one of the finest buildings in the city. Appropriately for a long-time seat of power, it commands the main square, Largo do Senado, with a classically symmetrical façade of white-plastered stone walls and twin rows of green-shuttered windows beneath a simple pediment bearing Macau's coat of arms.

This is the newest part of the building, dating from 1875, after a typhoon badly damaged the old senate, constructed in 1784. This in turn replaced the original headquarters of the senate which was founded in 1583. The Loyal Senate was composed of a group of leading citizens, appointed for life, whose duty was to assist the governor. At least that was how it worked in other colonies, but Macau was unique in having a governor in name only. The title was held by the captain-major of the Japan Voyage, who let the senators run the city while he went about amassing a fortune.

Thus when Francisco de Mascarenhas, the first full-time governor, took up office in 1623, he found the senate in firm control of Macau's affairs. He was one of the toughest men Lisbon ever sent to Macau, yet failed to shake the senate's grip. Like many of his successors, he was regarded as a 'political appointee' on a two- or three-year tour of duty. How could such a person deal with the Chinese authorities who held Macau in virtual fiefdom? The Chinese-speaking senators, with their lives invested in the city, had long experience of keeping the mandarins happy. Men like Mascarenhas despised the way they paid bribes and granted China judicial rights over the people of Macau, but the senate knew that the alternative was the threat of a border closed to food supplies and problems in Canton for Macanese merchants.

For most of the 17th and 18th centuries, the senate battled both the governor and the Jesuits, who had considerable power and influence, but eventually it became an anachronism. In 1833 Lisbon reduced the body to its present status as a municipal council. Today, members are appointed by a governor or elected. They hold weekly meetings to discuss such matters as public markets, parks and utility services in an imposing council chamber where portraits of past governors line the walls and crystal chandeliers hang from a coffered wooden ceiling. The chamber can be visited on certain occasions, such as at election time.

Most of the other interesting parts of the building are open to the public. The main door frames a memorable Macau scene. In front is the spacious foyer, with art gallery and government offices leading off to the right and left. Ahead is a noble archway, crowned with a banner proclaiming Macau's full name, and a wide stone staircase leading up to a wall embossed with a granite bas-relief of Our Lady of Mercy (possibly modelled on the saintly Queen Leonor) and topped with a small bell-tower.

Below, a pair of wrought-iron gates open on to a walled garden containing palm trees and flower beds. On the back wall are two cherubic gargoyles over an inoperative fountain, and on one wall a niche contains the statue of a youthful John the Baptist. On either side of the garden are busts of the poets Camões and João de Deus.

Panels of Portuguese blue-and-white tiles line the walls of the garden and staircases. They depict floral patterns, dolphins and angels. These *azulejos* are found all over Macau, in buildings old and new and as street name plaques. Interestingly, they are now made in a Chinese factory across the border.

Behind the Closed Shutters

Though it was past the siesta, the shutters of the high, narrow Portuguese windows of the Rua do Hospital remained shut; but as Abraham Biddle, key in hand, mounted two paved steps to the tall double front door, Thomas observed by the slight movement of an upper-floor shutter that though Macao houses sometimes wore an air of somnolence it should not be inferred from this that the people inside them were asleep. Just as small as the world of the foreign traders in China—though more settled, in that its inhabitants came and went only by birth and death—was Macao itself, a world in which it was prudent to keep shutters closed.

Before they were fully inside the hall two Chinese servants in white tunics hurried down from the upper floor, noiseless in neat black cloth slippers, the shape of which stood out markedly in the dim light against the white stockings and puttees in which their baggy black silk trousers were gathered. Without waiting for orders they began flinging open the shutters in the ground-floor rooms, although in fact there was little to see in them—being level with the street, they were conspicuously empty of possessions.

Upstairs other servants were opening shutters on all sides, filling the house with light, bringing its quiet old dignity to life.

They were standing in what William Urquhart had used as his living room. It was in complete contrast with the arid lower rooms, the life of a Macao house being conducted (with the exception of cooking) entirely on the upper floor. Persian carpets of appropriate sizes covered nearly every foot of floor space, out across the landings and into other rooms beyond. There were some good pieces of English furniture, but the larger cabinets and almeiras were Portuguese, ornately carved with pilaster and acanthus, with which were blended peonies and other Chinese motifs, masterpieces of the cabinet-maker's art. The room was large, stretching from the front of the house to the back, divided centrally by an arch decorated with some Chinese craftsman's painstaking imitation of Portuguese manueline. The arch, giving the room two distinct parts, enhanced it with a subtle intimacy.

Austin Coates, City of Broken Promises

The Governor's residence

On the upper floor, next to the council chamber, is the library containing old newspapers and books about China in English. (See Museums, Art Galleries and Archives, page 45.)

Macau's oldest private home used to be famous as the **Camões Museum**. Located in its own grounds next to the Camões Gardens and the Old Protestant Cemetery, it consisted of a main storey of large, high-ceilinged rooms around a central atrium, with an equally spacious basement. Stone stairs led to an imposing portico with its roof supported by two square Doric columns.

In 1785 it was rented from the owner, Manuel Pereira, by the **British East India Company** as a residence-cum-office for its committee president and a suitable place to lodge visiting British dignitaries. The British named the house Casa Garden and in the next half-century it was the scene of many parties, banquets and theatrical soirées. It also witnessed many discussions about the state of trade and the difficulties of dealing with the Chinese, particularly when the company played host to ambassadors such as Lords Macartney, Amherst and Napier, all of whom at different times failed to persuade China to sign a trade treaty. Their failure led to the emergence of private traders like Jardine, Matheson and Dent, who prospered by importing opium. When its monopoly was destroyed, the British East India Company's charter was repealed in 1833 and its officers moved out of the Casa Garden.

Lancelot Dent took it over for a few years, and when he moved to Hong Kong, the owner presented it as a dowry to Commander Lourenço Marques when he married Pereira's daughter. However, it proved too expensive to maintain and in 1885 was put up for sale. The French offered Ptc60,000, but the Macau Government, at the insistence of the British, refused to allow the deal to go through and bought it themselves at half the price. It was used as an ammunition depot, offices of the public works department and the government printing office until it was converted into the Camões Museum in 1960. The museum was closed in 1989. It was rebuilt according to the old plan by the Orient Foundation, which now has offices in some of the building, while most is given over to museum rooms and an art gallery. It is once again known as Casa Garden.

Although the founding of Hong Kong in 1841 and the subsequent departure of foreign merchants and money deprived Macau of most of its revenue, there were a few rich people left who indulged in a building sprèe. And fortunately there was a local architect of genius to do the work, although neither of his two masterpieces are open to the public. Nevertheless, their exteriors make them prime attractions for photographers.

The architect was **Jose Agostinho Tomas de Aquino**, a Macanese who had studied in Lisbon. When he returned in 1825, he quickly made a name for himself by building houses for Jardine and other merchants as well as a new cathedral and the Penha Hermitage (none of which have survived). Before his death in 1852 at the age of 48, he also built St Lawrence's church and the Salesian Institute. However, his real claim to fame is his palaces.

Aquino's client was Alexandrino Antonio de Melo, **Viscount of Cercal**, head of Macau's most prominent family. The viscount had bought a plot of land in the **Santa Sancha** district, on the ridge above the Praia Grande, and in 1846 he commissioned Aquino to build him a palace.

The result is a marvellous example of colonial architecture. The two-storey mansion faces the sea, allowing prevailing breezes to cool it in the hot, humid summers—as well as inviting good fortune, according to the priples of Chinese geomancy. The large portico between twin towers supports an open terrace outside the master bedroom, while the roof above sports a rounded pediment decorated with the Portuguese coat of arms.

The stone walls are inset with high windows and louvred wooden shutters. Over each window is a stucco moulding, and the flat Chinese roof is surrounded by low balustrades trimmed with baroque bas-relief. Today the shutters and trim are painted white and the walls are salmon pink, a requisite for government buildings. The palace is surrounded by landscaped gardens which complement its classical symmetry.

The viscount was so delighted with this palace that three years later he ordered another to be built to accommodate his overflowing family. The site was a choice spot on the Praia Grande promenade, the envy of all. No one today can doubt that it succeeded. Now the **Government Palace**, the building displays Aquino's gift for balance. Here again we find the stately entrance with a colonnaded veranda, but unlike at Santa Sancha there are three deep balconies on the upper floor, each framed with Corinthian columns.

A central pediment carries the national coat of arms, while the flags of Portugal and the governor fly on either side. The windows, smaller than those at Santa Sancha, have grey wooden-louvred shutters, while the walls are government pink.

The story of how both palaces became government property reflects the events taking place at the time. The viscount's heir was the multi-talented Baron of Cercal, a qualified engineer, an accomplished architect (he designed the Military Club, St Michael's chapel and the façade of Dom Pedro V), a linguist (he served as consul in Macau for France, Brazil, Belgium and Britain), soldier and conscientious citizen (he sat on innumerable councils). Possibly because of his many activities, he failed in business and lost the family fortune.

The 1875 typhoon devastated many buildings on the praia, including the governor's mansion. The baron saw a way out of his problems and leased the Praia Palace

Examples of Macau's Portuguese-inspired architecture, beautifully preserved at Lou Lim Ieoc (above right), St Joseph's Seminary (above) and St Dominic's Church (right)

to the governor. Six years later he was forced to sell it. The Santa Sancha palace was purchased in 1892 by British trader Lancelot Dent, who sold it to the government in 1923. (The interiors of both palaces are described in *Chronicles in Stone*, by S Davies.)

During this era, Macau society as well as visitors from Hong Kong had the chance to enjoy European culture in the **Dom Pedro V Theatre**. Built by the Macau Club, which had its statutes approved in 1859, this was the first European playhouse on the China coast and it soon became a stop on the international circuit for touring opera companies, theatre troupes and soloists from all over the world.

Among the Asian premieres staged in Macau were *The Barber of Seville* performed by an Italian company, *The Count of Luxembourg* by a Russian troupe and *The Daughter of the Regiment* by the French Opera Comique. In more recent times, the Dom Pedro V has been a venue for such artists as Benjamin Britten, Julius Katchen, Ruggiero Ricci and Helen Traubel.

The theatre was also the scene of anniversary tributes to St Francis Xavier and Vasco da Gama, diplomatic receptions and masked balls. Local theatre groups honoured the three Portuguese airmen who made the first flight from Lisbon to China in 1924 by putting on two plays, T*he Golden Key* and *The Embezzlement*. In the previous year, a troupe had raised money for the victims of the Tokyo earthquake—with the rather odd choice of a comedy called *Joys of the Home*.

After a period of decline, the theatre was totally renovated in 1977 and equipped with modern lighting and sound systems in order to stage the Crazy Paris Show. This regularly packed the Dom Pedro until it was transferred to the Lisboa Hotel. Today the theatre is being restored by the Orient Foundation.

The theatre shares the Largo de Sto Agostinho with St Augustine's church, the Jesuit-run Casa Ricci charity and Jesuit residence, St Joseph's Seminary, and the former mansion of Sir Robert Ho Tung (now a library). The façade, designed by the Baron of Cercal, is painted pale green with white stucco decoration. Four pairs of Ionic columns between arches support a pediment and the words 'Teatro Dom Pedro V' appear on stucco 'curtains' over the arches, which face a tree-filled courtyard.

In the late 19th and early 20th centuries, the theatre stood at one end of the fashionable ridge above the Praia Grande, while another green and white landmark stood at the other. This is the **Bela Vista Hotel**, one of the most popular sights of Macau.

The Bela Vista was built in the 1880s, partially on the foundations of the old Bomparto fort, and has had more lives than the proverbial cat. Its first owner was William Clarke, the English captain of the ferry *Heungshan* which plied between Hong Kong and Macau. He personally escorted passengers by sedan chair from the Inner Harbour wharf to the hotel, which was then named the Boa Vista (Good View).

Although it enjoyed an excellent reputation, the Boa Vista did not prove profitable and in 1901 Clarke put it up for sale. The French consul in Canton, on instructions from the governor-general of French Indochina, offered Ptc70,000. The French wanted a 'rest-and-recuperation' centre for their colonials, but rival colonials in Britain objected to any encroachment upon what they regarded as their own territory. The Macau Government was therefore ordered by London's old ally Lisbon to step in and take over the 'English' hotel. As there were no local buyers, the Santa Casa da Misericordia was persuaded to take it over 'for the good of the nation', according to their archives. There were plans to convert it into a hospital, but that proved too expensive, and from 1917 to 1923 it was used as a secondary school.

Finally, the Santa Casa handed it back to the government, which sold it in 1932 to a Macanese woman. She turned it into a boarding school for newly arrived cadets in the Hong Kong Government, who were required to spend several months in Macau learning Cantonese. From their reports, it seems they very much enjoyed their classroom setting.

The cadets moved out in 1937, but others from Hong Kong arrived four years later seeking refuge from the Japanese occupation. They made use of all available space in the hotel, including the terrace, for their sleeping quarters. When peace was restored, the perennial problem returned—what to do with the Boa Vista? The answer was to rent it out to the British NAAFI Military Club until 1950, during which time it was renamed Bela Vista (Beautiful View) and transformed again into a hotel.

With the growth of tourism in the 1970s the hotel attracted many guests, but it soon became obvious that it needed extensive renovation if it was to be viable. After much delay and dispute, the building was bought by the government, which signed a management agreement with Mandarin Oriental Hotels. The hotel reopened in 1992 with its familiar façade beautifully restored and the veranda ready for diners. The old rooms have been reduced to eight deluxe suites.

There are many other good examples of late-colonial architecture all over Macau. One is the Military Club, designed in 1870 by the Baron of Cercal along neo-classical lines. It has a spacious veranda, high shuttered windows and a pleasing façade. Another is the former home of Hong Kong tycoon, Sir Robert Ho Tung (who lived here during the Second World War), which now houses a library of Chinese books. It is a graceful neo-classical mansion with arched windows between white columns and cream stone walls. On the islands, the restored mansions on Taipa praia are also masterpieces of the genre.

Chinese Shop-houses, Macanese Terraces

While the rich and powerful residents of Macau were building spacious houses, the vast majority had to be content with blocks of crowded tenements. These two- or three-storey buildings became very common in cities along the South China coast during the mid-19th and early 20th centuries.

Their design was dictated by the lack of space available for the waves of peasant migrants from China who were in retreat from famine or in search of a better life. The tenements were made up of narrow rooms with high ceilings (often with cocklofts), which tended to be poorly lit and ventilated. Small rear courtyards enabled residents to hang their laundry, rear chickens and tend potted plants.

In many cases, the ground floor of the tenements was given over to a shop or workroom, with folding metal gates that were pushed aside during waking hours. The family would sleep upstairs in these shop-houses, but the real life of the community took place at street level.

Large numbers of shop-houses can be seen in the older districts of Guangzhou (Canton) and Shantou (Swatow), as well as in Hong Kong, but they seem to have survived with their commercial utility and social importance intact in Macau, and anyone interested in the life of the China Coast at the turn of the century should plan a stroll through one of the territory's 'Chinatowns'.

One of the best-preserved districts stretches along the **Inner Harbour**'s Rua das Lorchas and Rua do Almirante Sergio. True, some of the original tenements have been rebuilt with claddings of yellow or green tiles, and their ground floors are devoted to selling real estate or high fashion. But there are still many shop-houses occupied by ships-chandlers selling nets, hoists, capstans, compasses, anchors and other sea-going supplies.

Another community that manages to survive gentrification is the cluster of small streets below **Monte Hill**. Craftsmen have been working here since the late 16th century, when the Jesuits hired them to build St Paul's. At that time the area was close to the harbour, and there were shops to supply seafarers with shrines for their boats, barrels for their catch, buckets for swabbing the decks and lucky red paper for their festivals.

You can still see all these products being made in the ground-floor workshops in a triangle formed by Rua da Tercena, Rua Nossa Senhora do Amparo and Rua das Estalagens. In addition, there are wood-carvers fashioning camphor chests with inlaid marble or mother-of-pearl for clients in New York, London and Tokyo, along with makers of bamboo bird cages, washboards and household items.

Balconies combining Chinese and Portuguese features

Suggested Tour Itineraries

Although Macau is small, it can be confusing for visitors who have limited time to explore. The following itineraries cover the prime attractions of the territory and include some of the best restaurants. They can be followed individually or back-to-back. In general, the tours will be best appreciated on foot. However, we recommend that you take taxis or buses to get from the arrival wharf to the tour starting points.

Full descriptions of the attractions can be found elsewhere in the book.

Tour One
Peninsula Macau Take a taxi to Government Palace (although there is no entry to the public, take time to admire the exterior and the adjoining garden). Follow the Praia Grande waterfront, taking in the seascape and colonial mansions among the new high-rises. Turn right up the steep Rua Bomparto to Calcada da Penha. Once at the top, visit the chapel of Our Lady of Penha, brouse through the tourist shops and take in the panoramic views. Return to Bomparto and detour to the Bela Vista Hotel. Continue along the praia to Pousada de São Tiago. Follow the road round to the A-Ma Temple and Maritime Museum. If it is lunch or dinner time, proceed to A Lorcha or Barra Nova restaurants. Walk along the Inner Harbour road or return by bus or taxi.

Tour Two
Historic Downtown Take a bus or taxi to Leal Senado square. Visit the Leal Senado, Santa Casa da Misericordia and Tourist Office. Follow the main street, Avenida Almeida Ribeiro, to Rua Mercadores. Turn right past the Central Hotel and São Domingos Market to Rua São Paulo. Enjoy the façade of St Paul's. Proceed along Rua São Paulo to Camões Garden, the Old Protestant Cemetery and Casa Garden. Return by bus or taxi.

Tour Three
Northern Suburbs Take a taxi or bus to Kun Iam Temple. Cross the road to the Centro Comercial, with shops of traditional porcelain and furniture as well as antique shops. Proceed north on Avenida do Coronel Mesquita to

the Canidrome and the Lin Fong Temple. Take the Istmo Ferreira do Amaral to the China border. Return by bus or taxi.

Tour Four
São Lazaro Take a taxi to Guia fort and lighthouse. Walk down the Calcada do Paiol, past the Royal Hotel and Vasco da Gama Garden to Calcada São Lazaro. Stop to look at the beautifully-renovated houses around the church of São Lazaro. Return to the Avenida do Conselheiro Ferreira de Almeida and head north to Restoration Row. Turn left on Estrada Adolfo Loureiro to visit the Lou Lim Ieoc Garden. Return along the street to reach Avenida Sidonio Pais. Here you will find the Sun Yat-sen Memorial House and, a few blocks up the street, Balichao restaurant. Return by bus or taxi.

Tour Five
Taipa village Take a bus or taxi to Taipa village. From the bus terminus, stroll around the village streets, packed with traditional China coast houses, some converted into restaurants, others selling food products. Then, climb the small hill to the Carmel church and garden. Continue down the praia to visit the Taipa House Museum. Return by bus or taxi.

Tour Six
Coloane Village Take a bus or taxi to Coloane village square. Look at the small park with its European fountain. At the end of the square is the waterfront and a pier which is used by boats that commute across the channel to a nearby Chinese island. A little to the south is the chapel dedicated to St Francis Xavier, and beyond it the Tam Kong Temple. Return to Rua do Estaleiro, behind the temple, along tree-lined roads and some traditional China coast houses. There are two Chinese temples a small detour from the road, one dedicated to Kun Iam and the other to Tin Hau. Return by bus or taxi.

Alternatively, take the bus to Coloane Park to explore the walk-in aviary and nature trails that lead to Coloane Alto. This is a favourite place for picnics and panoramic views.

Two other institutions of the old China Coast thrive in Macau. One is the **Chinese medicine shop**, an excellent example of which is the Farmacia Tai Ning Tong on Rua de Cinco de Outubro, just off the main street one block from the Inner Harbour. It boasts an elaborately carved lintel and, in its cavernous depths, huge apothecary jars filled with substances animal, vegetable and mineral, showcases of deerhorn and cabinets with hundreds of small drawers filled with herbs which are mixed in the back of the shop.

Another complementary part of Macau's heritage is the **Macanese terrace house**, which illustrates the territory's hybrid culture. The best examples of this style of building are in the São Lazaro district.

The Macanese terraces are basically Chinese tenements which have been transformed with balconies of wrought-iron or stone balustrades, stucco reliefs around windows, and ornamental eaves and walls that are regularly given a pastel wash of green, cream or pale blue. The end result is sometimes fussy or garish, but the streets of São Lazaro show how attractive it can be.

To see for yourself, turn off Rua do Campo at Rua de João de Almeida (two blocks from the Royal Hotel), which becomes Calçada Igreja de São Lazaro. On the right is the new church of St Lazarus, on the left a three-storey apartment building with slim-columned balconies, green doors and shutters painted cream and brown.

Next door stands a choice example of gingerbread architecture. It is a library-bookshop, with colonnaded verandas, wrought-iron balconies, stuccoed capitals and a pseudo-Greek temple on the roof. The other buildings on this street are less lavish but just as lovingly restored as the terraces along cobblestoned Rua de Eduardo Marques. At the end of the Calçada Igreja de São Lazaro are stone stairs leading to Rua Sanches de Miranda, where several old mansions are being rebuilt.

From here it is a short walk to Monte fort, or you can return to Rua do Campo and continue a block to **Avenida do Conselheiro Ferreira de Almeida**. Here you will find some terraces which have earned international fame and a Pacific Area Travel Association Heritage Award. The buildings date from the 1920s when they were private homes. In the 1970s they were earmarked for demolition, but the government stepped in and bought them. Their interiors were completely gutted to create offices and are now occupied by the National Archives and National Library. At the same time, the frontages were restored so that the arched verandas installed on the upper floors match the street-level arcades. New ornamental balustrades were added to the roofs and the exteriors were painted cream and burnt sienna, a colour combination that mellows with age.

Drying joss sticks

Modern Macau

Since the late 1960s, Macau's economy has prospered through a boom in manufacturing and increased revenues from the casinos. To celebrate this coming of age, the *nouveau riches* have erected their monuments. Most are predictable skyscrapers, clad in tinted glass or painted in livid colours, largely devoid of grace or distinction. Few are more than concrete boxes.

There are some brilliant architects in Macau, but they work for clients who demand that every square metre of space pay its way. This is most evident in the new industrial zones that stretch between the old city and the Chinese border. The multistorey factories here produce a colourful variety of garments, toys, electronics and other products, but the buildings are uniform and uninviting.

In melodramatic contrast is the modern symbol of Macau, the Lisboa Hotel, which opened in 1970. According to popular legend, STDM, the gambling syndicate that built it, sent a team around the world to gather inspiration for its design. With roofs modelled on roulette wheels, scalloped balconies and walls of mustard-coloured tiles, the result qualifies as a dozen styles in search of an architecture, appalling to some, bizarrely appealing to others. See for yourself, and be sure to visit the casino even if you don't gamble.

The newest buildings tend to be rather featureless skyscrapers that distort the traditional skyline, but two of them are exceptional. The new Macau headquarters for the Bank of China is a massive grey tower that dwarfs the neighbouring Lisboa and can be seen from across the border. More imaginative are the offices of the Finance Department, which rise in art-deco splendour above the pink-stone colonial bank on the corner of the Praia Grande and main street.

However, it is the public works projects that dominate the construction scene. On the government's drawing boards are a variety of grandiose plans. One of the most significant for those who love old Macau is the multi-billion dollar 'urban development' of Praia Bay. Work has already begun on reclaiming land for a suburb, 1.7 million square metres (5.61 million square feet) in size, to contain houses, offfices, hotels, artificial lakes and a six-lane highway.

Other projects include a new ferry terminal, an enlarged container port and an industrial park alongside the Taipa–Coloane causeway. However, the major focus is on the international airport. Initiated in 1989, its cost—after a lot of upward readjustment—had been fixed at Ptc6.5 billion (US$835 million), which will be paid for by the government, STDM and investment by China and local companies.

The contracts are divided between a Portuguese-led consortium which will build the three-kilometre (1.85-mile) runway on piles in the sea off Taipa Island, and Chinese contractors who will reclaim land for the terminal and hangars. To appreciate the engineering challenge, visit the Chinese Cemetery on Taipa and look down on the site. At the same time, glance over at the Outer Harbour and consider the parallel project—a 4,700-metre (5,142-yard) bridge from the airport to the wharf, at an estimated cost of Ptc500 million (US$62.5 million). The airport is scheduled to open by mid-1995 and the bridge in 1993.

Gardens and Grottoes

With half a million people crowded into 9.7 square kilometres (six square miles), Macau is one of the most densely populated places on earth, but fortunately for both residents and visitors, choice corners of the territory's acreage are given over to public gardens that are open from dawn to dusk.

The **Camões Garden** is one of the most pleasant and interesting. It is situated next to the former museum and the Old Protestant Cemetery on a rocky promontory overlooking the Inner Harbour and Lappa Island. It features a natural grotto of large boulders, which today contains a heroic bust of the poet Luis Camões (1524–79). It is popularly believed that he lived in Macau the year it was settled and wrote some of his epic, *Os Lusiados*, here.

In the 18th century it became the grounds of the Casa Garden and a 'wilderness' for guests of the British East India Company to explore. It was also used by La Perouse, who built an observatory here. (See Explorers and Adventurers, page 70.)

The observatory has since been removed, but there is a Chinese pavilion where local people meet, play Chinese chess and read the newspapers. There are paths winding between thick groves of trees and bamboo, with secluded benches much favoured by young lovers. The section near the gate is filled with liana-draped banyans and, on most mornings, men airing their caged songbirds.

If the Camões Garden is a European stylization of nature, the **Lou Lim Ieoc Garden** is the Chinese representation. Located in the São Lazaro district on Estrada de Adolfo Loureiro, it was built in the 19th century by a wealthy Chinese merchant on the model of the classic Suzhou gardens.

Hidden behind a high wall is a courtyard and moon-gates which lead to a world in miniature made up of concrete 'mountains', bamboo 'forests' and a lotus-pond 'sea'. Linking them are paths which offer viewing and photo opportunities at every turn. In the middle of the pond, accessed by a nine-bend bridge (to deter evil spirits which move in straight lines) is a Western-style pavilion used for exhibitions. (Unlike the other gardens, an entrance fee of Ptc1 is charged every day except Sunday.)

The **Flora Gardens**, on Avenida de Sidonio Pais close to the Estoril Hotel, were also created in the last century, when they comprised the grounds of the Flora Palace, an aristocratic Portuguese mansion destroyed by fire in 1931. The gardens are landscaped in European style, with flower beds, exotic shrubs, a wide variety of trees (labelled in Latin and Chinese) and an ornamental pond complete with water-fowl. Where the palace once stood is a small zoo. Cages of monkeys, goats, birds and a brown bear that was a gift from China are ranged around a courtyard containing a circular fountain, built on a base of stone carp with dragon faces, and a bust of three-time governor, Tamagnini de Souza Barbosa, who held this position between 1918 and 1937. Steps lead up the slope to Guia Hill from behind the gardens.

Macau has several commemorative parks set off from the main streets, with benches for people who wish to relax or to eat their lunch. The best known is **Vasco da Gama Garden**. Located in front of the Royal Hotel, it features a bust of the great explorer.

The **St Francis Garden**, next to the barracks, consists of a series of terraces with trees and benches and a memorial shaped like a Martello tower, honouring the combatants of the First World War.

There are a number of gardens on Macau's rural islands of Taipa and Coloane. The **Carmel Garden**, in front of the Church of Our Lady of Carmel on Taipa, overlooks both the old village and the praia waterfront. It occupies a small hilltop with a fine lookout, landscaped flower beds and a fountain within a vine-covered bower that would not disgrace the finest Portuguese *palacio* or Arabian alcazar.

Much of the larger, less-populated island of Coloane is natural parkland, where you can follow dirt trails around the hillsides. **Coloane Park**, created by the Forestry Department, is now operated by the local council. Its special attraction is a net-roofed, walk-in aviary (next door to the 1999 Restaurant), which is home to more than 200 species of birds including the Palawan peacock and white-crested pheasant.

The park also has a lake with some resident black swans, a flower nursery, a children's playground with an old steam engine and trails up to the top of the hill for splendid views. (Admission to the park is free, but it costs Ptc5 to enter the aviary.)

The other parks on Coloane are run by the Clube Solagua. Both are usually open to members only, but occasionally the **Hac Sa recreational complex** hosts contests for water sports, tennis, volleyball, badminton, basketball and roller-skating, when spectators are welcome.

(above) *Camões Grotto*; (below) *relaxing in Camões Gardens*

Cemeteries

In Western countries, a cemetery usually earns its place on a tourist itinerary as the last resting place of some famous person. Colonial cemeteries, on the other hand, tend to qualify as 'corners of some foreign field' for more ordinary folk. Macau's **Old Protestant Cemetery** merits a visit on both counts.

It boasts the graves of artist George Chinnery (1774–1852) and Robert Morrison (1782–1834), the missionary who translated the Bible into Chinese. Other tombstones with famous names are those belonging to Henry John Spencer Churchill, Sir Winston's great-grand-uncle and the senior British naval officer in the China Seas when he died here in 1840, and Joseph Adams, a naval lieutenant and grandson of George Washington.

The cemetery was opened in the 1820s (not 1814 as stated on the entrance) and was the first piece of land sold by the Portuguese to non-Portuguese. There are quite a few earlier dates on the graves because some of the remains were transferred here from sites outside the city.

Of the 150 graves, about 100 are British and 50 American, with a handful of Europeans, including Anders Ljungstedt, a Swedish trader who wrote the first history of Macau in 1834. Among the more elaborate tombs are those of opium traders like James Innes and Captain John Crockett. Less ostentatious are the graves of young sailors who 'fell from aloft', were killed by pirates or died of illness. Among the latter were some who sailed with Commodore Perry, who spent the winter of 1853 in Macau and Hong Kong after having delivered his ultimatum to Japan to open her doors to foreign trade.

By 1858, lack of space made it necessary to establish the **New Protestant Cemetery** in the north of the city (at the intersection of Avenida do Coronel Mesquita and Rua Silva Mendes). To date, little research has been done concerning the people buried here, but there is one tomb with a sad claim to fame. It holds the remains of the China-born Lutheran missionary Dr Daniel Nelson and those of his wife, son and daughter. In 1948, setting off on a planned visit to the United States, they boarded the plane that crashed during the first recorded aerial hijack attempt. (See Seaplane Sagas, page 141.)

The **Roman Catholic Cemetery of St Michael's**, well-tended and beautifully landscaped, surrounds the charming neo-gothic chapel. Its most famous tomb is that of Mesquita, the hero of 1849 (see Mong-ha fort, page 68). There are also sepulchres containing several generations of Macanese families as well as members of Catholic missions active in China. Most interesting for an outsider, however, are the bi-cultural tombs, with European angels guarding Chinese omega-shaped graves.

The majority of Chinese graves are found in the **United Chinese Cemetery** on the eastern shores of Taipa, spread over the hillside facing the estuary and the site of the new airport. The cemetery entrance has a wall of brightly coloured tiles under a roof with upswept eaves. Inside is a ten-metre (30-foot) statue of Tou Tei, god of the earth, robed in bright yellow and carrying a staff.

Tou Tei towers over a garden of moon-gates, classical pavilions and images of Buddhist and Taoist deities, beyond which are the terraces of graves. During festivals that include ancestor worship, the cemetery is packed with people sweeping family graves, burning joss sticks and having picnics.

All the cemeteries are open from dawn to dusk.

"There is None More Loyal"

There have been many lavish parties in Macau, but the most extravagant on record must be the ten weeks of festivities in the summer of 1642 that marked the restoration of the Portuguese monarchy—and coincidentally the end of Macau's Golden Age.

The Duke of Braganza had become King João IV of Portugal on 1 December 1640, following a dynastic struggle that ended Spain's 60-year rule of the Iberian peninsula. The new government found itself with no army, an insignificant navy and very little in the treasury. It had also to re-establish control of its far-flung colonies.

Macau was in particular danger, with the Spaniards in nearby Manila eager to acquire a gateway for China trade. It was vital that a Portuguese deliver news of the restoration as soon as possible, and a Macanese trader, then in Lisbon, was despatched.

After a tortuous journey on British and Dutch ships, he arrived in Macau on 30 May 1642, to find the city in a state of near civil war, with the governor and the Jesuits battling the bishop and the mendicant orders of Augustinians, Dominicans and Franciscans.

Swords were sheathed, and they called a patriotic truce to unite with hundreds of fellow citizens on 31 May when they pledged their allegiance to King João on a great silk-canopied stage set up in Leal Senado Square.

It seems that the entire population of 40,000 joined in the ensuing celebrations, which were recorded by Father Marques Moreira, a local apostolic notary. 'All evils vanished,' he wrote, as Macau indulged in an orgy of ostentation, taking to the streets 'richly dressed in costly garments bedecked with jewels, which made the scene appear like a city of kings'.

The Portuguese wore costumes of blue taffeta with gold roses and buttons, and their hats were covered with gold chains, rubies, pearls and diamonds. Their slaves sported uniforms of the finest silk, their horses were caparisoned in silver mesh, and their palanquins curtained with lace.

Almost continuous rain failed to dampen the festivities. Bonfires flared from every hill, and wax torches lit up St Paul's and other buildings. The entertainment included Portuguese-style bullfights, tilting and equestrian ballgames in the square; displays by Chinese musketeers; pageants along streets hung with coloured lanterns; music, masques and masquerades.

Macau's international community was much in evidence, with a parade of Chinese dressed as mandarins, kimono-clad Japanese, Persians in bejewelled turbans, and Dutch merchants in capes and breeches, all accompanied by an honour guard of mounted German archers.

St Paul's, which contemporary visitors called the finest church in Asia, was the scene of a magnificent *Te Deum* and a thanksgiving that was truly resounding—because of the rain, the traditional rifle volleys were fired in the nave!

Yet even as they gloried in the spectacle, those taking part were all too aware that this could be Macau's last celebration. As Father Moreira noted, 'The city became as if it had returned to its former condition...when at the height of its wealth and glory, [it was] supplied by channels of gold and rivers of silver'. That had been before Japan closed its doors to trade in 1639 and the Dutch had captured Malacca two years later. True, Macau remained China's sole entrepôt for international trade, but the Portuguese would soon be reduced to the role of middlemen for other Western merchants.

But no matter. In the summer of 1642, the people of Macau devoted themselves to welcoming a new age in Portugal. Understanding the plight of the new king, they sent a gift of arms and money. João IV was obviously appreciative of the offering as well as the show of allegiance, and in return he granted the city its proud title: *Nao ha outra mais leal*—There is none more loyal.

(Moreira's full account appears in Charles Boxer's *Seventeenth Century Macau*)

Library in Leal Senado

Recommended Reading

History

Boxer, C R, *Fidalgos in the Far East 1550–1770* (Martinus Nijhoff, The Hague, 1948. Reprinted Oxford University Press, 1968)
Boxer, C R, *The Portuguese Seaborne Empire* (Hutchinson & Co, London, 1969)
Boxer, C R, *The Christian Century in Japan* (University of California Press, 1967)
Boxer, C R, *Francisco Viera de Figueiredo: a Portuguese Merchant-Adventurer in South East Asia* (Martinus Nijhoff, The Hague, 1967)
Boxer, C R, *Four Centuries of Portuguese Expansion, 1415–1825* (University of California Press, 1969)
Boxer, C R, *The Great Ship from Amacon: Annals of Macau and the Old Japan Trade, 1555–1640* (Instituto Cultural, Macau, 1988)
Boxer, C R, *Jan Compagnie in War and Peace 1602–1799* (Heinemann, Hong Kong, 1979)
Boxer, C R, *South China in the Sixteenth Century, Narratives of Galeote Pereira, 1550–1575* (Hakluyt Society, 1953)
Boxer, C R, *Seventeenth Century Macau* (Heinemann, Hong Kong, 1984)
Braga, J M, *A Seller of 'Sing-Songs'* (Journal of Oriental Studies, Hong Kong, vol 6, 1961–64)
Braga, J M, *With the Flowery Banner: Some Comments on the Americans in Macau and South China* (N T Fernandes, Macau, 1940)
Braga, J M, *The Western Pioneers and their Discovery of Macau* (Portuguese of Hong Kong Institute, Macau, 1949)
Braga, J M, *China Landfall* (Karel Weiss, Hong Kong, 1956)
Coates, A, *Macao and the British 1637–1842* (formerly titled *Prelude to Hong Kong*, Oxford University Press, Hong Kong, 1987)
Coates, A, *A Macao Narrative* (Oxford University Press, Hong Kong, 1987)
Collis, M, *Foreign Mud* (Faber & Faber, London, 1946)
Eames, J B, *The English in China 1600–1843* (Curzon, London, 1974)
Hibbert, C, *The Dragon Wakes* (Penguin, 1970)
Ljungstedt, A, *Historical Sketch of the Portuguese Settlements in China* (Boston, 1836)
Montalto de Jesus, C A, *Historic Macao* (Oxford University Press, Hong Kong, 1984, reprinted from the 1926 edition)
Morse, H B, *Chronicles of the East India Company, Trading in China 1635–1834* (Clarendon, Oxford, 1926)

Pires, Tome, *The Suma Oriental* (edited by Armando Cortesao, Hakluyt Society, 1944)
Souza, G B, *The Survival of Empire: Portuguese Trade and Society in China, 1630–1754* (Cambridge University Press, 1986)
Teixeira, M, *The Japanese in Macao in the XVIth and XVIIth Centuries* (Imprensa Nacional, Macau, 1974)

Religion

Cooper, M, *Rodrigues the Interpreter* (Weatherhill, Tokyo and New York, 1974)
Teixeira, M, *The Church of St Paul* (Studia, Lisbon, 1979)
Teixeira, M, *The Fourth Centenary of the Jesuits at Macau* (Salesian School, Macau, 1964)

Travellers' Tales

Hamilton, A, *A New Account of the East Indies* (Argonaut, London, 1930, reprint of a diary first published 1727)
Hunter, W C, *Bits of Old China* (Kegan Paul, Trench, London, 1885)
Hunter, W C, *The 'Fankwae' at Canton* (Kegan Paul, Trench, London, 1844)
Mundy, P C, *The Travels of Mundy in Europe and Asia 1608–1667* (Hakluyt Society, London, 1919)

Literature

Camões, L V, *The Lusiads* (Penguin, 1952)
Coates, A, *City of Broken Promises* (Oxford University Press, Hong Kong, 1988, reprinted from the 1977 Heinemann edition)

Arts and Architecture

Briggs, T, *Old Macau* (South China Morning Post, Hong Kong, 1984)
Davies, S, *Chronicles in Stone* (Department of Tourism, Macau, 1985)

(following pages) *Macau historian Father Manuel Teixeira in his study at St Joseph's Seminary*

Graca, J, *Fortifications of Macau* (Department of Tourism, Macau, 1984)
Guillen-Nunez, C, *China Trade Paintings* (Instituto Cultural, Macau, 1986)
Hugo-Brunt, M, 'An Architectural Survey of the Jesuit Seminary Church of St Paul's' (*Journal of Oriental Studies*, Hong Kong, July 1954)
Hugo-Brunt, M, 'The Parish Church of St Lawrence' (*Journal of Orental Studies*, vol 6, 1961–64)
Hutcheon, R G and Bonsall, G, *Chinnery: The Man and the Legend* (South China Morning Post, Hong Kong, 1975)
Hutcheon, R G, *Souvenirs of Auguste Borget* (South China Morning Post, Hong Kong, 1979)
O'Neill, J, *Macau* (Collection of pen-and-ink drawings, Macau Mokes, Hong Kong, 1987)
Orange, J, *The Chater Collection: Pictures Relating to China, Hong Kong and Macao, 1665-1860* (Thornton Butterworth, London, 1924)

Tourism and Travel Guides

Braga, J M, *Macau: A Short Handbook* (Tourism Department, Macau, 1970)
Clemens, J, *Discovering Macau* (Macmillan, Hong Kong, 1983)
Clewlow, C, *Hong Kong, Macau and Canton* (Lonely Planet, Melbourne, 1981)
Davies, S, *Macau* (Times Editions, Singapore, 1986)
Davies, S, *Viva Macau* (Macmillan, Hong Kong, 1980)
Davies, S, *Fodor's Guide to Hong Kong and Macau* (Random House, 1992)
Fleming, I, *Thrilling Cities* (Reprint Society, London, 1964)
Guillen-Nunez, C, *Macau* (Oxford University Press, Hong Kong, 1984)
Lockhart, S, *Hong Kong* (Insight Guides, Hong Kong, 1988)
Monteiro, F, *The Renascence of Macao* (Public Works Department, Macau, 1924)
Papineau, A J G, *Papineau's Guide to Hong Kong and Macau* (Andre, Singapore, 1977)
Rolnick, H, *Macau: A Glimpse of Glory* (Ted Thomas, Hong Kong, 1980)
Simpson, C, *Asia's Bright Balconies* (Angus & Robertson, London, 1962)
Teixeira, M, *The Protestant Cemeteries of Macau* (Department of Tourism, Macau, 1984)
Teixeira, M, *A Precious Treasure in Coloane* (Department of Tourism, Macau, 1982)
Teixeira, M, *The Chinese Temple of Barra* (Department of Tourism, Macau, 1982)
Thomas, E M, *The Macau Mokes Guide to Macau* (Macau Mokes, Macau, 1990)

Gambling

A-O-A, *Macau Gambling Handbook*
Okuley, B and King-Poole, F, *Gamblers Guide to Macau* (South China Morning Post, Hong Kong, 1979)
O'Neal-Dunne, P, *Roulette for the Millions* (Sidgwick & Jackson, London, 1971)

General

Cremer, R D, ed, *Macau: City of Commerce and Culture* (University of East Asia Press, Hong Kong, 1991)
Davies, S, *Macau Miscellany* (Derwent Communications, Hong Kong, 1992)

(following pages) *Annual summer fireworks festival*

Practical Information

Hotels and Guesthouses

There is something for everyone in Macau from imperial suites to backpacker board, all at rates about half those in Hong Kong. The best hotels are as well-equipped and attractively appointed as Hong Kong's five-star properties, while Macau has far more moderately priced hotels, with clean, comfortable rooms, helpful staff and restaurants serving Western food.

There is a good choice of budget one-star hotels and *villas*, or guesthouses. Most of these are located around the Inner Harbour or downtown and provide airconditioning, television, flasks of hot water for coffee or tea, attached bathrooms or showers, and sometimes restaurants.

Although Macau lists three *pousadas*, or Portuguese-style inns, only the São Tiago has historic foundations, and none is government-operated, unlike those in Portugal.

All but the cheapest hotels have English-speaking staff and booking offices in Hong Kong. They accept major credit cards, with MasterCard and Visa being the most popular. Budget rooms are best booked in Cantonese. Assistance is available from staff in the tourist office at the Macau wharf.

In most hotels, room rates are the same for single and double occupancy, and guests are usually required to pay in advance. A 10 per cent service charge and 5 per cent tax are added.

NB. Most hotels offer up to 20 per cent discounts on weekdays.

INTERNATIONAL FIRST CLASS (PTC750–1,400)
Bela Vista 8 Rua do Comendador Kou Ho Neng. Tel 573-821.
This century-old landmark has been rebuilt as a deluxe hotel with eight suites and a Portuguese restaurant. The famous terrace is the ideal place for leisurely meals and drinks against a backdrop of Praia Bay and Taipa Island. Bookings can be made through offices of Mandarin Oriental Hotels.

Hotel Grandeur Rua Pequim, Macau.
350 rooms. Chinese and Italian restaurants, revolving restaurant/nightclub on top floor, indoor pool and sauna, business centre, beauty salon. This four-star hotel is managed by China Travel Service (Hong Kong) and can be booked through CTS in Hong Kong (Tel 853-3888).

Holiday Inn Macau Rua Pequim, Macau. Tel 781-707; fax (853) 781-711.

451 rooms, including Executive Club floors. Chinese and Italian restaurants, coffee shop, Fun Pub, indoor pool, health club, business centre. The four-star hotel is in the new Outer Harbour hotel district, convenient for the wharf and casinos. Bookings can be made in Hong Kong (Tel 736-6955) or Holidex reservations.

Hyatt Regency Taipa Island. Tel 831-234; tlx 88512 HYMAC OM; fax (853)320-595. 353 rooms including 14 suites. Portuguese restaurant, coffee shop, lounge, casino, ballroom, business centre, function rooms, outdoor swimming pool, gardens, jogging track, tennis and squash courts, all-purpose court for team sports, fully-equipped gymnasium, spa with sauna, massage, beauty parlour, open-sided pavilion-style restaurant, shuttle bus to the wharf. Superb resort facilities and decor combine the best of classic Iberia and traditional China. Bookings can be made in Hong Kong (tel (852)559-0168) and through Hyatt International worldwide.

Mandarin Oriental Ave da Amizade. Tel (853)567-888; tlx 88588 MACEX OM; fax (853)594-589.
438 rooms, including 32 suites. Shopping arcade, Chinese restaurant, Western grill, coffee shop, bar, casino, two outdoor swimming pools, gymnasium, tennis and squash courts, sauna and massage, beauty parlour, business centre, banquet rooms, shuttle bus to the wharf. This hotel is worth a visit just for the reproductions of Portuguese art from the Age of Exploration and some fine blue-and-white tile murals. The Guia Bar, with deep leather armchairs and views of the harbour, is possibly the most elegant in town. Bookings can be made in Hong Kong (Tel 548-7676) or through Mandarin Oriental offices worldwide.

New Century Estrada Almirante Marques Esparteiro, Taipa Island. Tel 831-111; fax (853)832-222.
Situated at the end of the Macau–Taipa bridge, opposite the Hyatt Regency, this is a hotel that impresses with its sumptuous lobby, variety of Eastern and Western restaurants, top-class disco/karaoke, gorgeous ballroom and large array of recreational facilities, such as an outdoor pool, gymnasium, squash and tennis courts, sauna and massage, bowling and snooker. Bookings can be made in Hong Kong (tel 548-2213).

Pousada de São Tiago Fortaleza de São Tiago, Ave da Republica. Tel 78111; tlx 88376 TIAGO OM; fax (853)553-170.
23 rooms including two suites. Western restaurant, dining terrace, outdoor pool, chapel, bar, function room. With its 17th-century foundations, fabulous architecture, reproduction period furniture and spectacular views, the São Tiago is a prime tourist attraction as well as a hotel. (Details page 67.) Hong Kong booking (tel 540-8180).

Pousada Ritz Rua da Boa Vista. Tel 339-955; tlx 88316 RITZOM; fax (853)317-826. 31 rooms, half with balconies. This hotel, built into the hill behind the Bela Vista, has restaurants, saunas, a business centre and other facilities. Bookings can be made in Hong Kong (tel 739-6993 and 540-6333).

Royal Estrada da Vitoria. Tel 552-222; tlx 88514 ROYAL OM; fax (853)563-008. 380 rooms including 15 suites. Shopping arcade, squash courts, health club, beauty parlour, indoor pool, slot machine hall, Western, Chinese and Japanese restaurants, karaoke bar. The Royal is well-located and famous for its food. Bookings can be made in Hong Kong (tel 548-6333) and through Dai-Ichi offices worldwide.

Westin Resort Hac Sa, Coloane Island. Tel 871-111; fax 871-122. Dramatically situated on a headland overlooking the beach, this resort boasts striking architecture, 208 rooms with deep balconies, Portuguese and Cantonese restaurants, indoor and outdoor pools, a health club, eight tennis courts and a casino. The Macau Golf and Country Club has a clubhouse on the top floors of the hotel while the 18-hole golf course is built into the wooded hills behind it. Bookings can be made at any Westin office.

ONE OF A KIND!
Lisboa Ave da Amizade. Tel 577-666; tlx 88203 HOTEL OM; fax (853)562-285. 1,120 rooms (Ptc600-850) and suites. Cantonese, Shanghainese, Chiu Chow, Japanese, Korean, Portuguese and continental restaurants, six bar lounges, shopping arcades, casino, swimming pool, sauna, health club, billiards room, disco, Crazy Paris Show revue. The Lisboa is not really a five-star hotel, but rather a landmark of modern Macau, with a bizarre design and bewildering assortment of facilities. Bookings can be made in Hong Kong (tel 559-1028).

MIDDLE OF THE MARKET (PTC300-750)
Beverly Plaza Ave Dr Rodrigo Rodrigues. Tel 337-755; tlx 88345 HTLBP OM; fax (853)308-878.
Suites, executive rooms, apartments. Shopping arcade, Chinese and Western restaurants, lobby bar. This new hotel is managed by China Travel Service, which has its offices in the same building, making it convenient for people travelling to China. Bookings can be made in Hong Kong (tel 540-6333).

Fortuna Rua de Cantao, Macau. Tel 572-588; fax (853) 73061.
402 rooms. Chinese and Western restaurants, nightclub, health club. This three-star hotel in the Outer harbour caters mostly to Hong Kong visitors.

Roadside shrine

Guia 1 Est Engenheiro Trigo, Guia Hill. Tel 513-888; tlx 88736 GUIA OM; fax (853)559-822.
89 rooms including 10 suites. Chinese restaurant, coffee shop, disco, karaoke, wharf shuttle bus. Bookings can be made in Hong Kong (tel 770-9303).

Kingsway Rua Luis Gonzaga Gomes, Outer Harbour. Tel 702-888; fax (853)702-828.
Close to the ferry terminal, this is a medium-priced hotel with 420 rooms, restaurants and casino. Bookings can be made in Hong Kong (tel 571-1886).

Matsuya 5 Est São Francisco. Tel 575-466; fax (853)568-080.
Western restaurant, terrace, karaoke. The main attraction of this hotel is the superb view of the Outer Harbour. Bookings can be made in Hong Kong (tel 368-6181).

Metropole 63 Rua da Praia Grande. Tel 88166; tlx 88356 CTS OM; fax (853)330-890.
110 rooms. Managed by the China Travel Service and well-located in the heart of the town. Bookings can be made in Hong Kong (tel 540-6333).

Mondial Rua de Antonio Basto. Tel 566-866; fax (853)514-083.
141 rooms, including six suites. Chinese and Portuguese restaurants, bar, disco. The Mondial consists of an old wing of one-star quality and a handsome new 75-room block that is suitable for international visitors. Hong Kong bookings (tel 540-8180).

New World Emperor Rua de Xangai, Outer Harbour. Tel 781-888; fax (853)782-287.
New hotel with 405 rooms, European-style bistro and first-class Cantonese restaurant, as well as a hot-pot dining room. Bookings can be made through any New World International Hotels' office.

Pousada de Coloane Praia de Cheoc Van, Coloane Island. Tel 328-143; tlx 88690 PDC OM; fax (853)328-251.
22 rooms. Dining terrace, Portuguese restaurant, bar, swimming pool, transport to/from the wharf. Half surrounded by a forest of pines and tropical trees and overlooking Macau's best beach, the Pousada is packed with Hong Kong families during the summer. It is a perfect retreat for overnight stays or meals in the excellent restaurant or on the spacious terrace. Bookings can be made in Hong Kong (tel 540-8180).

Presidente Ave da Amizade. Tel 553-888; tlx 88440 HPM OM; fax (853)552-735.
333 rooms. Western, Chinese and Korean restaurants, lobby bar, Skylight nightclub/disco, sauna, karaoke. Popular for its Outer Harbour waterfront location and nightclub with a floor show of British strippers. Hong Kong bookings (tel 525-6873).

Sintra Ave D João IV. Tel 385-111; tlx 88324 SINTA OM; fax (853)567-769.
236 rooms. European restaurant, bar-lounge, sauna. The Sintra is favoured by regular Hong Kong visitors because of its downtown location, views of the bay and efficient service. Bookings can be made in Hong Kong (tel 540-8028).

BUDGET HOTELS (PTC100-300)

Central Ave Almeida Ribeiro. Tel 777-000.
160 rooms. Chinese restaurant. Situated on the main street, what was once the gambling and prostitution centre of Macau is now a convenient budget hotel.

East Asia 1 Rua da Madeira. Tel 572-631; fax (853)389-748.
98 rooms. Chinese restaurant, lounge. Recently renovated and with English-speaking staff, this is one of the best one-star hotels in the heart of old Macau. Bookings can be made in Hong Kong (tel 540-6333).

Grand 146 Ave Almeida Ribeiro. Tel 579-922; fax (853)511-591.
90 rooms. Chinese and Western restaurants, nightclub. Across the street from both the Kam Pek and Macau Palace floating casinos, the Grand is a natural for gamblers.

Ko Wah Rua Felicidade. Tel 75452.
30 rooms. On the third floor of a building in the old red-light district, the Ko Wah is clean and bright with comfortable rooms and English-speaking staff. No meal service.

London 4 Praca Ponte e Horta. Tel 83388.
46 rooms. This small, modern hotel is pleasantly located in a square off the Inner Harbour waterfront. The rooms are fine, but there is no meal service.

Peninsula Rua das Lorchas. Tel 318-899; fax 344-933.
123 rooms. This new hotel, on the upper floors of a modern building built on the seawall of the Inner Harbour, has attractive rooms; the best have marvellous views of the harbour. A restaurant and nightclub can be found in the building. Bookings can be made in Hong Kong (tel 833-9300).

GUESTHOUSES (PTC40-150)

There are dozens of *villas*, or guesthouses, but few cater to foreigners and little English is spoken. Try: Capital (Rua Constantino Brito 3; tel 571-782), Ka Va (Val S João 5; tel 574-022), Kam Loi (Ave Infante D Henrique 34; tel 77608), Kuan Heng (Rua Ponte e Horta 4; tel 573-629), Nam Long (Rua Dr Pedro Jose Lobo 30; tel 81042), Nam Pan (Ave D João IV 8; tel 572-289). Ask the Tourist Office for help.

Macanese façades

Restaurants

It is impossible to categorize Macau's non-Asian restaurants very precisely because of the culinary interchange that has resulted in Macanese dishes and international grills appearing alongside Portuguese, Continental, Italian and even African food on most menus.

Prices at all restaurants are reasonable, with an average three-course meal (excluding wine) costing Ptc80–100, inclusive of 10 per cent service. Exceptions are noted. Service is invariably pleasant (with no hustling!) if sometimes a little slow.

Unless mentioned, credit cards (particularly MasterCard and Visa) are accepted, and reservations are not necessary. Opening hours are 11 am or noon to about 11.30 pm, usually with an afternoon break, as noted.

Macanese/Western

A Galera Lisboa Hotel, new wing, third floor. Tel 577-666, ext 1103. One of the most attractive dining rooms in town, with elegant Portuguese decor (fine blue-and-white tiles line the walls), interesting views of the São Francisco fort, a club-like bar, evening piano music and imaginative menu of first-class Portuguese and Macanese dishes. Prices about 50 percent above average. Open 12.30 pm–2.30 pm, 7–11 pm.

A Lorcha Rua do Almirante Sergio 289, on the Inner Harbour waterfront road, close to the A-Ma Temple and Maritime Museum. Tel 313-193. A new restaurant, as trim as the sailing boat it is named after, with some of Macau's best Portuguese and Macanese food. Try the delicious casseroles. Open 1 pm–3 pm, 7–11 pm.

Afonso's Hyatt Regency Hotel, Taipa Island. Tel 831-234 ext 1921. Beautifully designed with indoor-garden decor, pleasant views and good Portuguese food. Occasional evening entertainment. Open 12 noon–3 pm, 7–11 pm.

Afonso III Rua Central 11, behind the Leal Senado. Tel 586-272. The owner/chef is the original Afonso, whose daily specials feature Portuguese dishes rarely served in Macau's restaurants, and at bargain prices. Favourites include paté the way his grandmother made it. Open 12 noon–11 pm.

Balichao Hoi Fu Building, 93A–99 Estrada das Cacilhas. Tel 566-000. One of the most elegant and inviting restaurants in town, with great decor and an extensive menu that includes the best of Portuguese and Macanese dishes, such as *lacassa* with local shrimp paste (*balichao* in Portuguese). Open 12 noon–3 pm, 7–11.30 pm.

Barra Nova Rua do Almirante Sergio, on the Inner Harbour waterfront. Tel 512-287. A homely place with excellent Portuguese/Macanese dishes, including silver codfish. Open 11 am–11 pm.

Café Luso Rua Central 33. Tel 570-413. A popular café with locals for Portuguese, Italian and Macanese dishes, including seafood pizza and the tastiest squid in town. Prices are at the lower end of average. No credit cards. Open 12 noon–11 pm.

Fat Siu Lau Rua da Felicidade 64. Tel 573-585. Opened in 1903, this was the first European restaurant in Macau and it continues to be one of the best. The three-storey building (with Iberian façade and interior) is in the old red-light district. Famous dishes are roast pigeon and African chicken. No credit cards. Open 11 am–1.30 am.

Flamingo Hyatt Regency Hotel, Taipa Island. Tel 831-234 ext 1834. A marvellous pavilion-style restaurant overlooking a lake (with mandarin ducks) and gardens. The Portuguese country decor and atmosphere more than compensate for occasional kitchen lapses, and the complimentary loaf of fresh bread is alone worth a visit. Most dishes are Macanese. Open 12 noon–2.30 pm, 7–10.30 pm.

Fortaleza Grill Pousada São Tiago, Ave Republica. Tel 78111. The menu contains some delicious Portuguese and Macanese dishes (such as vegetable soup and seafood casserole) and the service is immaculate, but the fort setting and 18th-century style colonial dining room are what make dining here unique. Prices are about double the average. Open 12 noon–3 pm, 7–11 pm.

Galo Rua do Cunha 47, Taipa village. Tel 327-318. A two-storey village house converted into a Portuguese-style restaurant with such Macanese touches as Chinese-hat lampshades. The menu contains Macanese favourites and regional Portuguese dishes like lamb on a skewer à la Madeira. Prices are below average, with main courses about Ptc25. No credit cards.

Henri's Galley Ave Republica 4. Tel 562-231. A long-standing favourite with local Portuguese and Chinese, plus Hong Kong regulars. Specialities include African chicken, curried crab, Portuguese fried rice and Macau's best spicy prawns. Also some pavement tables. Henri Vong is a great host.

Leong Un Rua de Cunha 46, Taipa village. Tel 327-387. Despite the name, this is an Italian restaurant with pizzas and pasta, plus some Macanese dishes. Most agreeable. Open 11 am–11 pm.

Chinese cafés on Inner Harbour road

Moçambique Rua dos Clerigos 28, Taipa village. Tel 321-475. Given its former imperial connections, it is not surprising to find an African restaurant in Macau. Here the specialities are Angolan dishes like *matapa* (spinach, saffron and shrimps) and African chicken, with spices baked in the bird. No credit cards. Closed afternoons.

1999 Coloane Island. Tel 328-291. Great location next to a walk-in aviary, with continental dishes and local favourites like African chicken and Portuguese cod (*bacalhau*). Open 12 noon–11 pm. Closed Mondays.

Panda Rua Carlos Eugenio 4–8, Taipa village. Tel 327-338. A wide selection of Macanese and Portuguese dishes served in a series of rooms decorated in garden-style. Open 11 am–10.30 pm.

Pinocchios Rua do Sol 4, Taipa village. Tel 327-128. The first Western restaurant on Taipa and still famous for its curried crab, steamed shrimp and roast lamb. No credit cards. Open 12 noon–10 pm.

Portugues 16 Rua do Campo. Tel 375-445. Cosy, unpretentious and always to be relied on for excellent *feijoada* Brazilian stews and the best codfish *bacalhau a bras* in town. Service comes with a smile and prices are at the low end of average.

Pousada de Coloane Praia de Cheoc Van, Coloane Island. Tel 328-144. Portuguese-style restaurant with spacious terrace overlooking the beach and sea. A great getaway, with fine Portuguese food, including the best stuffed squid in town. The Sunday buffet is a sumptuous feast at a bargain price. Closed afternoons.

Praia Grande Praca Lobo d'Avila (off Rua da Praia Grande). Tel 973-022. Perfectly located with some of the best views of the Praia Grande Bay. The decor is pure Iberian, with white arches and red-stone floors. The menu is country Portuguese, with Macanese features like *dim sum* à la Praia Grande: Chinese baskets of sardines, codfish pies, shrimps and chicken. Open 12 noon–12 midnight.

Safari Patio do Cotovelo 14, off Ave de Almeida Ribeiro. Tel 574-313. Located in the heart of town, with a varied menu of Macanese dishes and grills. Open 9 am–1 am.

Solmar Rua da Praia Grande 11. Tel 574-391. A centrally-located gathering place for Portuguese residents, the Solmar has been a local institution for many years, and sometimes the food and service reflect this. Best bets are the baked Portuguese chicken and the codfish. No credit cards. Open 11 am–11 pm.

One of a Kind
The Riquexo Sidonio Pais 69, in Park 'N Shop. Tel 76294. The food is delivered here each morning from private kitchens. All dishes are purely Macanese (with a strong Chinese element, for instance *minchi*—minced pork and diced potatoes pan-fried with soy sauce—and duckling cooked in its own blood). Prices are incredibly low, with wine almost as cheap as at the supermarket. The Riquexo opens at noon and the most popular dishes go quickly; home-made desserts and cakes are served in the afternoon. Closed evenings and the first Monday of the month. No credit cards.

One of Another Kind!
Fernando's Tel 328-264. This restaurant is popular with those who seek the ultimate in informality. In fact, it is hard to find in its spacious garden behind the façade of simple sheds that line Hac Sa beach. Marvellous Portuguese meals are served under high ceiling fans in a red-brick pavilion. Open 12 noon–9.30 pm. No credit cards.

Chinese and other Asian
While most visitors will devote their eating hour to Macanese meals, the city offers a wide range of other dining possibilities. Naturally, most residents and Hong Kong visitors opt for Chinese food at one of the hundreds of restaurants that specialize in Cantonese or other provincial cuisines. In addition, there are restaurants serving food from neighbouring Asian countries. The following are the best known:

Chiu Chau Lisboa Hotel. Tel 377-666. This opulent banquet room caters to the many locals and visitors with roots in Chiu Chow (Chaozhou), a county in Guangdong Province. They give it top marks for the grand diversity of fine dishes. Open 11 am–12 midnight.

Dynasty Mandarin Oriental Hotel. Tel 567-888 ext 3821. A favourite among locals for Cantonese meals in a setting of red lacquer panels and tasselled lanterns. The food rivals Hong Kong's best (specials include minced pigeon and boneless chicken with scrambled eggs). Prices at the top end of average. Open 8 am–3 pm, 6–11 pm.

Fook Lam Mun Ave da Amizade 63. On the Outer Harbour waterfront. Tel 386-388. According to locals, this is the best Cantonese kitchen in town, with a huge menu, agreeable setting and prices slightly above average. Open 7.30 am–12 midnight.

Furosato Lisboa Hotel. Tel 577-666 ext 1137. A branch of the renowned Japanese group, with *sushi, tempura, teppanyaki* and other favourites, plus a Korean menu. Open noon–3 pm, 6–11 pm.

Ginza Royal Hotel. Tel 568-412. With its classic decor of plain blond wood, tatami rooms and super food, Ginza is understandably popular with Japananese visitors. Prices are relatively high for Macau, but very low compared with Japan or Hong Kong. Open 12 noon–3 pm, 6 pm–12 midnight.

Korean Presidente Hotel, Ave da Amizade. Tel 569-039. A great place for *bulgogi* grilled beef and other Korean favourites, served with traditional courtesy in an authentic setting. Open 12 noon–3 pm, 6 pm–12 midnight.

Long Kei Largo do Leal Senado 7B. Tel 573-970. Located in the main square, this vintage Cantonese restaurant has a menu of 359 dishes, plus many specials (in Chinese only) and a noisy, cheerful ambience. Open 11 am–11 pm.

Nova Koka Ferreira do Amaral 21, near the Royal Hotel. Tel 568-993. A pleasant, cheap, country-style Thai restaurant, with a good choice of dishes and friendly service, although little English is spoken. Open 11 am–6 am.

Royal Canton Royal Hotel. Tel 552-222. Very popular among locals for morning *dim sum* snacks and family parties, with an extensive menu and efficient service. Open 8 am–12 midnight.

Shanghai 4 5 6 Lisboa Hotel, new wing. Tel 388-474. The best Shanghainese restaurant in Macau, renowned for its eel with bamboo shoots, beancurd with minced beef, and Peking duck. Prices are average for Macau, making it a bargain compared to other places. Very popular, so it is usually crowded. Open 11 am–1 am.

Thai Rua Abreu Nunes, close to the Royal Hotel. Tel 573-288. A good example of the city's growing number of Thai restaurants that cater to the tourists as well as the thousands of Thais who work here as hostesses and masseuses. The menu is extensive, prices are reasonable and the service is with a big smile, if little English. Open 12 noon–3 pm, 6 pm to 6 am.

Macau is famous for its salted fish

Useful Addresses & Telephone Numbers

International Offices of the Macau Tourist Information Bureau

Australia: 449 Darling St, Balmain, Sydney, NSW 2041
   Tel (02)555-7548, (008)252-448; fax (02)555-7559
Canada: Suite 305, 1530 West 8th Ave, Vancouver, BC V6J 1T5
   Tel (604)736-1095; fax (604)736-7761
   5059 Yonge St, Ontario M2N 5P2
   Tel (416)733-8768; fax (416)221-5227
Great Britain: 6 Sherlock Mews, Paddington St, London W1M 3RH
   Tel (071)224-3390; fax (071)224-0601
Hong Kong: 3704 Shun Tak Centre, 200 Connaught Rd, Central
   Tel (852)540-8180; fax(852) 559-6513
Japan: 4/F, Toho Twin Tower Bldg, 5-2 Yurakucho
   1-chome, Chiyoda-ku, Tokyo 100
   Tel (03)3501-5022/23; fax (03)3502-1248
New Zealand: PO Box 42-165, Orakei, Auckland 5
   Tel (09)520-3317; fax (09)520-3327
Philippines: 402 Copacabana Apartel, 30 P Lovina St, Pasay City, Metro Manila
   Tel (632)831-8711; fax (632)834-0847
Portugal: Avenida 5 de Outubro 115-5/F, 1000 Lisbon
   Tel (1)769-864/6
Singapore: 11-01A PIL Building, 140 Cecil Street, Singapore 0106
   Tel (65)225-0022; fax (65)223-8585
Thailand: 150/5 Sukumvit 20, Bangkok 10110/GPO Box 1543, Bangkok 10501
   Tel (662)258-1975; fax (662)258-1975
USA: 3133 Lake Hollywood Drive, PO Box 1860, Los Angeles, CA 90078
   Tel (213)851-3402, (800)331-7150; fax (213)851-3684
   Suite 316, 70A Greenwich Ave, New York, NY 10011
   Tel (212)206-6828; fax (212)924-0882
   630 Green Bay Rd/PO Box 350, Kenilworth, Illinois
   60043-0350 Tel (708)251-6421; fax (708)256-5601
   PO Box 22188, Honolulu, Hawaii 96922
   Tel (808)538-7613

Macau

Macau Government Tourist Office, Largo do Senado Tel (853) 315-566; fax (853)510-104

Tourist Information, Ferry Terminal Bldg. Tel (853)555-424
Emergency Telephone Numbers: General Emergency 999
                                      Ambulance 577-199
                                      Police 577-3333

TRAVEL AGENTS IN HONG KONG/MACAU

Macau Able Tours
    Ka On Bldg, 8 Connaught Rd, Hong Kong. Tel (852)545-9993
    5 Travessa do Padre Narciso, Macau. Tel (853)89798
Macau Asia
    Chung Ying Bldg, 20 Connaught Rd W, Hong Kong. Tel (852)548-8806
    23 Rua de Praia Grande, Macau. Tel (853)593-844
Macau Star
    Rm 18, 2/F Cheong Ning Bldg, Tsuen Cheong Centre, Tsuen Wan, Hong Kong. Tel (852)417-4600
    Rm 511, Tai Fung Bank Bldg, 34 Ave, Almeida Ribeiro, Macau. Tel (853)558-855
China Travel Service
    CTS Building, 78 Connaught Rd, Hong Kong. Tel (852)853-3533
    63 Rua de Praia Grande, Macau. Tel (853)782-331
Estoril Tours
    333 Shun Tak Centre, Connaught Rd, Hong Kong. Tel (852)559-1028
    G/F, New Wing, Hotel Lisboa, Macau. Tel (853)573-641
International Tourism
    Cheong Tai Commercial Bldg, 60 Wing Lok St, Hong Kong. Tel (852)541-2011
    9 Travessa do Padre Narciso, Macau. Tel (853)975-183
Macau Tours
    287 Des Voeux Rd, Hong Kong. Tel (852)542-2338
    35 Ave Dr Mario Soares, Macau. Tel (853)385-555
Sintra Tours
    Shun Tak Centre, Hong Kong. Tel (852)540-8028
    Sintra Hotel, Macau. Tel (853)710-373
South China
    8/F Mandarin Bldg, 35 Bonham Strand, Hong Kong. Tel (852)815-0208
    15 Ave Dr Rodrigo Rodrigues, Macau. Tel (853)781-811

(These travel agencies offer tour and reservation services in Macau as well as excursions to Zhongshan.)

(following pages) Fishing nets in Praia Bay

Chronology

Macau

1557	Macau settled
1582	Matteo Ricci studies in Macau
1585	Senate established
1603	St Pauls church opened
1622	Dutch invasion repelled
1642	Celebrations of Restoration
1625–64	Manuel Bocarro casts cannons for Macau and China
1705–15	Rites Controversy in Macau
	Western traders allowed limited access to trade in Guangzhou
1762	Jesuits expelled from Macau
1779	Captain Cook's ships visit Macau after his death in Hawaii
1785	Casa Garden rented to East India Company
1787	La Perouse in Macau
1808	British occupy Macau for three months
	Robert Morrison translates bible into Chinese
1825–52	George Chinnery in Macau
1828	Jardine and Matheson company
1834	British East India Company ceases operations
1835	Fire destroys Monte Fort, Jesuit College, St Paul's Church
	Foreign merchants move to Hong Kong
1844	First Sino-American treaty signed
1848	Governor Amaral assassinated, Chinese invasion thwarted by Mesquita
1853	Commodore Perry in Macau
1877	Sino-Portuguese recognizes Macau as Portuguese territory, cedes Taipa and Coloane to Macau
1894–96	Sun Yat-sen in Macau
1937	Pan Am completes first scheduled US–China flight
1941–45	Macau neutral in war, population doubles with refugees
1966	Communist riots
1987	Sino-Portuguese agreement to return Macau to Chinese sovereignty on 20 December 1999

Asia

1497	Vasco da Gama reaches India
1510	Portugal captures Goa
1511	Portugal captures Malacca
1513	Jorge Alvares lands in China
1524	Ambassador Pires dies in China
1549–51	Francis Xavier in Japan
1552	Xavier dies on China coast
1571	Nagasaki granted to Jesuits
1597	26 Christians martyred in Nagasaki
1603	Tokugawa Ieyasu becomes Shogun
1600–10	Matteo Ricci in Beijing
1619	Dutch East India Company in Batavia
1638	Portuguese expelled from Japan
1642	Dutch capture Malacca
1644	End of Ming Dynasty/beginning of Manchu/Ch'ing (Qing)
1662–1722	Reign of (Kangxi) K'ang Hsi emperor
1665	Death of Adam Schall in Beijing (at court since 1621)
1660–88	Ferdinand Verbiest at court in Beijing
1736–95	Reign of (Qianlong) Ch'ien Lung emperor
1762	British capture Manila (returned to Spain in 1763)
1784	Empress of China first US ship to visit China
	Rapid growth of opium trade
1834	Lord Napier's China mission fails
1841–42	Sino-British (Opium) War
1842	China cedes Hong Kong to Britain, opens treaty ports at Guangzhou Xiamen (Amoy), Fuzhou, Ningpo and Shanghai
1854	Commodore Perry forces Japan to open ports to foreign trade
1863–1908	Robert Hart creates and heads China Customs Service
1868	Meiji Restoration
1904–05	Russo-Japanese War
1911	Fall of Qing Dynasty and founding of the Republic of China
1949	Communist victory in China
1966–76	Cultural Revolution in China
1978	China opens doors to foreign investment and tourism

Europe/America

1419	Henry the Navigator launches fleet to look for fabled Cathay
1498	Treaty of Tordesillas divides all Catholic missions between Spain and Portugal
1549	Society of Jesus founded by Loyola and Xavier
1580	Union of Portuguese and Spanish crowns under Madrid
1588	Great Armada
1640	Restoration of Portuguese crown
1662	Wedding of Charles II of England and Catherine of Braganza, cementing Anglo-Portuguese alliance
1702–13	War of Spanish Succession (victory for Britain and new colonies in Canada)
1755	Lisbon earthquake
1756–63	Seven Years War (France loses Indian colonies to the British, who gradually expand control of the subcontinent)
1759	Pombal decrees expulsion of the Jesuits from Portuguese empire
1773	Boston Tea Party (with tea shipped through Macau)
1776	American independence
1789–1815	French Revolution and Napoleonic Wars
	Old regimes return in Europe
	America advances westward
	South American independence victories
1822	Brazil gains independence with Portuguese Prince Peter crowned emperor
1848	Liberal revolts throughout Europe
	Decline of Austrian Empire
	Unification of Germany
	Industrial Revolution
1910	Portugal becomes a republic
1914–18	World War I
1939–45	World War II
1989–90	Collapse of Communism in Eastern Europe

Seaplane Sagas

Visitors assume, and most residents believe, that the international airport now under construction will bring Macau into the Airborne Age for the first time. However, on two occasions the territory has already made aviation history—as the place where the first scheduled flight from America to China touched down, and the site of the first aeroplane hijack.

The story begins in 1924 with the arrival of the *Patria* from Portugal. In fact, the single-engine Breguet seaplane was forced by a typhoon to ditch in China after its historic ten-week journey, and the three Portuguese aviators spent several days being fêted in Hong Kong before reaching Macau.

There was some poetic justice therefore when, on 29 April 1937, Pan Am's *Hong Kong Clipper* flying boat splashed down in the Outer Harbour (where the Mandarin Oriental Hotel now stands), completing the first scheduled flight from the west coast of the United States to the Asian mainland. The plane was refuelled and took off for Hong Kong, its original destination, which had delayed granting landing permission in deference to Pan Am's British rival, Imperial Airways (the forerunner of British Airways).

While airlines from around the world made Hong Kong an aerial hub and gateway to China, Macau remained an optional port of call until the Pacific war broke out. As a Portuguese territory, Macau was neutral and, although blockaded by the Japanese, was not invaded—until 16 January 1945, when an American bomber appeared over Macau. Its target was the airport fuel depot, which the Americans feared could be used by the enemy.

After the war, the airport was rebuilt. Pan Am resumed occasional flights, but the main arrivals were Catalina seaplanes operated by fledgeling Cathay Pacific Airways. Their prime purpose was transporting gold between Hong Kong and Macau, where it could be legally traded as Portugal was not a signatory to the Bretton Woods Agreement, which banned its sale.

Many stories were told about these fabulous cargoes. Temptation was irresistible and, on 16 July 1948, four local Chinese joined 22 passengers and crew on board the seaplane *Miss Macau*. One of the pirates held a gun to pilot Cramer's head and ordered him to vacate his seat. Cramer refused. In the ensuing chaos, the ringleader panicked, shot the pilot and the plane crashed into four fathoms of muddy water in the Pearl River estuary. Fishermen picked up one of the thieves, whose account made international headlines as the first-known aeroplane hijack.

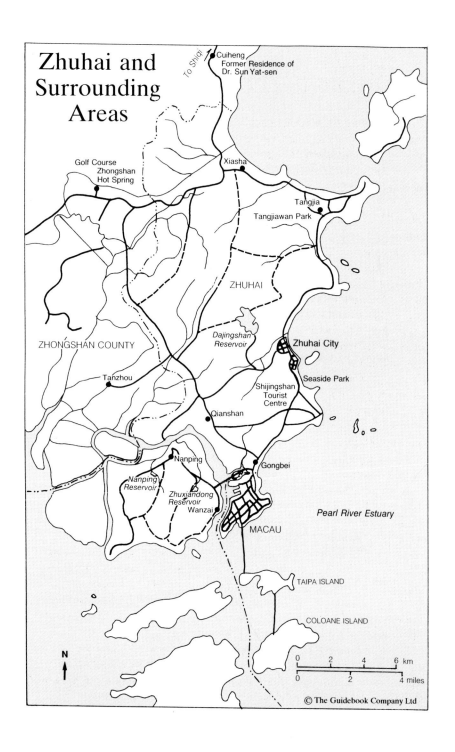

Excursions to Zhongshan and Zhuhai

The most popular day excursions from Hong Kong to China begin with a voyage to Macau. From the Macau wharf it is only a few minutes' drive to the Chinese border, where visitors are subjected to Macau departure procedure before entry formalities to China. Once on the other side, you can enjoy a convenient slice of traditional and modern Chinese life.

This is the county of Zhongshan (before 1911 known as Heungshan, afterwards Chungshan, and now spelt in pinyin), a well-chosen window on China for Western tourists, as it has been an entrepôt for trade and ideas between East and West for over four centuries.

Before 1557 the people of Heungshan, on the southwestern shore of the Pearl River estuary, lived in relatively properous obscurity. Their soil was enriched by river silt and the major town of Shekkei (now officially called Shiqi) was a busy inland port and market centre, far beyond the attention of Peking. Thus the imperial court paid scant attention when the Portuguese settled on a tiny peninsula in Heungshan which they named Macau. But the presence of overseas barbarians soon had its effects on the local people. As Macau developed into a booming entrepôt for China's foreign trade with Japan and Europe, the merchants of Canton made their fortunes selling silk, porcelain and other luxury goods in exchange for Japanese silver and spices from the Indies.

The merchants and mandarins of Heungshan also prospered. There is no evidence that Macau had been ceded by treaty, and it is most likely that the Portuguese came to an agreement with the Chinese whereby they paid for Macau with rent and customs duties.

In addition, the neighbouring Chinese were able to sell food and building materials to the settlers and, because the Portuguese refused to do manual work, farmers and artisans moved to Macau. One profound result was the first culinary interchange of East and West. The Portuguese introduced to China peanuts, sweet potatoes, lettuce, green beans, pineapples, papayas, shrimp paste and spices from India and Africa, as well as coffee and wine. In return they adopted Chinese rhubarb, celery, ginger, soy and tangerines (so named after their successful transplanting in Tangiers). The Chinese were the cooks in Macau and they taught the Europeans the benefits of quick-frying food to seal in the flavour. And, most historically important, the Portuguese discovered the delights of drinking tea.

At the same time, the Chinese helped to refine the lifestyle of the Portuguese and later Europeans by making available silks and other fine fabrics which were vastly superior to the coarse, heavy cloth worn in Europe. Western architecture was also affected by Chinese examples of high-ceilinged rooms and courtyards.

Tower-house Villages

Seen from the tour bus as it speeds along the highway, they look like mirages. Why else should there be small European forts, complete with turrets, scattered among the paddy fields of Zhongshan? Unfortunately, few tourists manage to get off the main roads to find out. If they did they would discover not only three- and four-storey fortresses, but small replicas of New York's Woolworth Building or buildings crowned with mock-Moorish domes and all manner of echoes of alien architecture.

Some Chinese guides maintain that they were built to protect the village from bandits, which might have been one advantage, but the real source of the towers is part of the 19th-century emigrant story. Tens of thousands of young Chinese from Zhongshan left to make their fortune overseas; some of those who succeeded returned and showed off their new affluence by building taller and fancier houses than their neighbours. Competition was keen and some of the villages have a veritable mini-Manhattan of high-rises.

The most famous contest, however, was between two families who lived in nearby villages. The Kwok and the Ma clans each welcomed home a young man who had made good, and to celebrate they built some of the tallest towers in the country. In fact, Mr Kwok and Mr Ma in 1917 had created in Shanghai two of the biggest retail and trading empires in Asia— Wing On and Sincere—which continue to compete in Hong Kong.

European ideas spread more slowly, but their effect was far-reaching. Some of the Chinese who worked in Macau were converted to Christianity; others gained a knowledge of the world beyond China, which in traditional Chinese maps was reduced to a vague fringe around the Middle Kingdom.

With a window to the West in Macau, natives of Heungshan became the first Chinese to migrate en masse to Western countries. The first groups departed in 1820 and many more followed. Where they went and what they accomplished is well illustrated in the Sun Yat-sen Memorial Hall in Shiqi. Maps show Heungshan migrants settling in countries throughout the world, from South America to Scandinavia, South Africa to New Zealand.

Many migrants suffered horrendous conditions in overseas gold mines, on the railways and in squalid Chinatowns. However, some prospered and returned home to build ostentatious tower-houses and mercantile companies. Equally important, young Chinese returned with Western ideals of democracy.

An opposition movement was spearheaded by Sun Yat-sen, who left his home in Heungshan to organize the revolution which toppled the Manchus in 1911. In his honour, the county was renamed Chungshan, or Zhongshan (Sun Yat-sen was also known as Sun Chung-shan, or Zhongshan). The 20th century has seen more upheavals in the area. It suffered considerable casualties during both the Second World War and the 1949 revolution. Much worse was the Cultural Revolution, when all Chinese with overseas connections were considered suspect. Since just about everyone in Zhongshan had family abroad, this was a dark time.

Today, in contrast, Zhongshan is enjoying a new era of prosperity, thanks to investments by overseas Chinese and the burgeoning tourist industry. Zhongshan County supports a population of about 1.3 million in its 1,780 square kilometres (687 square miles). It is still basically agricultural, producing over 50 different crops. Rice is the main crop, followed by sugar-cane, vegetables and fruit such as lychees and mangoes. Throughout the countryside there are duck farms and fish hatcheries, with fishing communities along the coast.

Increasingly there are modern industries, particularly in the Special Economic Zone of Zhuhai and in Shiqi. The main products are building materials, textiles, Western medicines, artificial flowers, processed food, electronic components, glass and bicycle parts. A large number of the new factories, hospitals and apartment blocks have been built with funds from overseas Chinese whose ancestral home is Zhongshan. These foreign cousins are now very welcome as visitors, and a special government office helps to track down families for those in search of their roots.

Getting There

Most visitors arrive in Zhongshan on package tours which include transport from Hong Kong to Macau, and transfer by bus to the border. The tours can also be arranged, at a lower cost, in Macau.

For golfers, businessmen and other individual travellers, there are more direct routes. The Hong Kong China Hydrofoil Company, Hong Kong (tel 523-2136), has three daily trips by jetcat to Zhuhai from the Hong Kong China Ferry Terminal in Kowloon. The 80-minute trip costs HK$120 on weekdays, HK$130 on weekends and holidays. In addition, Chu Kong Shipping, Hong Kong (tel 547-6538), runs four round-trips a day by jetcat from the Hong Kong China Ferry Terminal to Zhongshan Harbour, near Shiqi. The fare is HK$152. Prices include the HK$22 departure tax.

Dr Sun Yat-sen

The man who is today probably the most revered modern Chinese hero, Sun Yat-sen, was born in 1866 (the Year of the Tiger) in the village of Cuiheng (formerly written Tsui Hang), about 30 kilometres (19 miles) north of Macau, where his father once worked as a tailor. Like tens of thousands of young men from the area, Sun Yat-sen sought his fortune overseas. At the age of 13 he sailed to Honolulu, where his elder brother had settled, and studied at the British Missionary School and Oahu College.

In 1883, when he was 17, Sun returned to his home village a changed person. He had been converted to Christianity and was inspired by the ideals of Western democracy, which he attempted to teach to the peasants of Zhongshan. This made him unpopular with the local agents of the Manchu court, so he decided to continue his studies in Hong Kong.

Sun enrolled in the Faculty of Medicine at Queen's College (later Hong Kong University) and in 1892 was one of the British colony's first Chinese graduates. The same year he was baptised into the Protestant church. His first medical post was in Macau, where he worked (without the necessary Portuguese licence) at the Kiang Vu Hospital and at his own clinic, where he treated the poor without pay. At the same time, he wrote articles for the *Echo Macanese* advocating better education for the children of Zhongshan, aid to the farmers and the suppression of opium smoking.

The mandarins across the border recognized the rebel potential in Dr Sun and put pressure on the Macau authorities to expel him. Sun decided to face the enemy head on and in 1894 went to Canton, where he set up the Revive China Society, aimed at forcing the Machus to reform their rule in favour of the people. The Sino-Japanese War had just ended with China's humiliation, and some soldiers based in Canton mutinied because they had

Visas

Members of package tours travel on a group visa and need only advise the travel agent of their names, passport numbers and nationalities at least one day before departure. Individuals can obtain visas very easily from China Travel Service or other travel agents. (see Useful Addresses, pages 127 and 129.) Prices begin at HK$150 and increase as processing time decreases. Four hours is the minimum.

not been paid. The Society gave them support, which led the authorities to crush the mutiny and order Sun's arrest.

Sun evaded the police and escaped to Honolulu, whence he sent memorials to the Chinese court demanding political reform. He then sailed for London. In October 1896, in a bizarre plot which made headlines around the world, Sun was kidnapped in broad daylight and imprisoned in the Chinese Embassy. Spurred by Sun's former Hong Kong professor, Dr James Cantlie, the British press forced Parliament to demand his release.

Free again, Sun went to Tokyo where he spent the next ten years organizing anti-Manchu Chinese exiles into revolutionary societies. Then he travelled through Europe and the United States to form similar societies and gather support from liberal Westerners. One American journalist described 'the presence of an unusually self-possessed mind, as well as of a very strong character steeled against adversity'.

Sun's revolutionary programme stressed the need for 'giving free rein to people's talents and bringing agriculture into full play'. However, it was his call to overthrow the Manchu dynasty which became the priority of his followers in China. Their plan for an armed uprising in Wuhan was discovered by the authorities in the autumn of 1911, which forced the rebels to attack before Sun could get back from the United States.

By the time he reached China, the Manchu empire was no more. Sun was proclaimed 'Father of the Revolution' and named provisional president of the new republic. Meanwhile the country was thrown into political and economic chaos as revolutionary factions and opportunistic warlords battled for power.

Sun Yat-sen was persuaded to retire from office in 1912 and was reduced to a symbol and spokesman for the Nationalist Government. For the last 13 years of his life he travelled around his war-torn country, preaching the ideals that had led to the revolution to those who now had no time for them.

Tours and Touring

You can hire a car with a driver in Macau or at the border for private touring. Prices are negotiable and you need a Chinese speaker to get around. For backpackers, there are plenty of buses.

Tour itineraries vary, but all include a ride through Zhuhai and a visit to Sun Yat-sen's birthplace in Cuiheng. Most tours stop at a farming village where tourists are invited to visit the locals' homes. (They are paid by China Travel Service to keep their homes clean, but it nevertheless offers a vignette of rural life in southern China.)

Tour prices also vary. The cheapest are run by China Travel Service, but those available from local travel agents are more convenient. The former charge HK$740 per person on weekdays, HK$770 at weekends. Zhongshan is also included in two-day packages with one night in Macau, and in tours of three or four days that continue on to Shiqi, Foshan and Guangzhou.

Zhongshan

Cuiheng

Situated about 30 kilometres (19 miles) from Macau and 29 kilometres (18 miles) from Shiqi, this is a national shrine to Sun Yat-sen. Sun was born here in 1866 and in 1892 he returned to build a house for his parents. Like some houses still to be found in Macau and Hong Kong, the **Sun Yat-sen Home**, (Zhongshan *guju*) combines Chinese and European features. The front has seven-arched verandas along both storeys and challenges ancient superstition by facing the 'unlucky' west. The interior is in traditional Guangdong style, with high-ceilinged rooms, ancestral plaques, gilded carving and heavy blackwood furniture including a Chinese matrimonial bed. In the courtyard is the well of the original house and a silk tree planted by Sun with Hawaiian seeds.

Across the tree-shaded courtyard is the new **Sun Yat-sen Museum**. The museum consists of light, airy rooms ranged around a patio, each with displays concerned with the life and times of the man. All labels are in Chinese, English and Japanese, and video displays playing in different parts of the museum offer commentaries in all three languages. The museum is worth an hour or more. Also in the memorial park is the Sun Yat-sen Memorial High School, with blue-tiled roofs, which was built in 1934. It has about 700 students.

Shiqi

The chief town of Zhongshan, Shiqi (formerly spelt Shekkei) has been an important market centre and inland port for 800 years. The town, which is 61 kilometres (38 miles) from Macau and 79 kilometres (49 miles) from Canton, has a population of about 100,000 and sits astride the busy Qi River (Qijiang), where a cantilever bridge opens at mid-afternoon and at midnight—or when a ship's captain pays for extra service. The river presents interesting views, with sampans, small freighters, ferries and floating restaurants (open until very late at night) moored along the shore. Restaurants and night markets line the riverbank.

Symbol and landmark of the city is the Ming-Dynasty **pagoda** atop the hill close to the heart of town. It stands in a heavily wooded park where the walkways are paved with Qing-Dynasty tombstones. The pink and white pagoda has an interior winding staircase and at night is garlanded with bands of red and green lights. Nearby is the restored **Xishan Temple**, which consists of prayer halls on each side of a courtyard, plus a library of rare Buddhist literature.

Shiqi has a host of new buildings including apartments, textile factories and an impressive new hospital, mostly financed by Hong Kong Chinese. The most attractive is the **Sun Yat-sen Memorial Hall**, built for US$1.3 million by a Hong Kong construction tycoon in the mid-town park. Completed in 1983, it consists of a building with three pagoda-shaped yellow-tiled towers. Inside is an auditorium with 1,400 seats and extensive exhibition halls. These display Zhongshan's products, an excellent review of Sun Yat-sen's life and times (with only Chinese captions) and a comprehensive survey of the approximately 500,000 Zhongshan natives who live overseas.

Many tours include a visit to one of Shiqi's **kindergartens**, where the children give a charming song-and-dance show, and the guide details the government's school system.

For a one-time visit to China, Shiqi also offers a glimpse of the busy bicycle-packed streets and open-fronted shops typical of southern Chinese country towns.

Zhuhai

One of the first four Special Economic Zones (SEZ) to be set up in 1980—with liberal laws to attract foreign investment—Zhuhai grew from its original 13 square kilometres (five square miles) to the present 121 square kilometres (46 square miles), including offshore islands and the border town of Gongbei.

The population is about 150,000, with 30,000 in the main town of Xiangzhou. Zhuhai has proved itself a successful SEZ, with many factories (mostly owned by Macau or Hong Kong Chinese) producing textiles, medicine, electronic equipment, computer discs, pottery, lacquer furniture and an award-winning beer produced under the supervision of Stella Artois.

The main industry, however, is tourism. Tens of thousands of Chinese from all over the country come to pay their respects to Sun Yat-sen and to visit Zhuhai's glamorous resorts and well-equipped fun-fairs. They also go on shopping sprees in the large department stores crammed with foreign and Chinese products, and take each other's photograph against the background of Macau.

Sports and Entertainment

Zhongshan has become a playground for Chinese tourists, who flock to the big dippers, carousels and boating ponds of **Pearl Land amusement park**. For overseas visitors, the favoured recreational opportunities are two championship golf courses. Both are professionally designed and offer facilities and challenges that rank with the best in Asia.

The **Chung Shan (Zhongshan) Golf Course**, close to the Hot Springs Resort, was designed by Arnold Palmer's company and opened in 1984. It is a 72-par, 5,991-metre (6,554 yard) course of rolling hills, streams and sand-traps. A second 18-hole course, designed by Jack Niklaus, is being added in 1993. The clubhouse was designed by a Philippine company: the walls have rich wooden panelling, the furniture is high-grade rattan and the surroundings are elegant. Green fees are HK$450 a day for 18 holes during the week, HK$600 for a full day. The course is closed to visitors at weekends and during holidays. Caddies (most of them young women) can be hired for HK$100 a round and clubs are also available for HK$100 per round.

There is a resident pro, well-supplied pro shop and up-market health spa. The club can be reached from Macau in about an hour, or golfers can take the jetcat to Zhuhai and arrange for a club car to collect them. There are rooms for rent and the **Chung Shan Hot Springs Hotel** is close by for overnight accommodation. For bookings and transport arrangements, call the club's Hong Kong office at 504 Pedder Building, 12 Pedder Street (tel 521-0377).

The **Zhuhai International Golf Club** was established by Japanese interests in 1985. It is located on the coast, close to the border and Zhuhai ferry wharf. The 72-par, 6,380-metre (6,980 yard) course is wonderfully laid out in a long valley, with large sand-traps, lakes and woods. The clubhouse is a Japanese version of an antebellum mansion of the American South, with neo-classical pillars and spacious verandas. It is attractively furnished and offers a restaurant, bar, pro shop and elegant spa.

Green fees are HK$400 a day during the week, HK$600 at weekends and on holidays. Caddies can be hired for HK$100 per round, and a set of clubs for HK$100. For bookings in Hong Kong, telephone 721-3848.

Besides golf, most hotels offer tennis courts and swimming pools, while shooting and horse-riding are available at some. Evening entertainment is limited to karaoke, discos and occasional hotel floor shows, and there are a number of dance-halls in Shiqi.

Practical Information

Hotels and Restaurants

The following hotels are most frequently chosen by visitors for an overnight stay. Their restaurants are used by tour groups. Rooms for single or double occupancy are in the moderate range of HK$230-430, with up to a 20 per cent discount on weekdays.

Chung Shan Hot Springs Hotel Zhongshan. Tel 22911; tlx 44828. About 24 kilometres (15 miles) from Macau.
350 rooms in low-rise blocks and villas. Huge Chinese restaurant, Western dining room, pool, tennis courts, horse-riding, shooting range, shopping centre, nearby golf course. (For bookings in Hong Kong, tel 521-0377.)

Zhuhai Resort Zhuhai. Tel 23718; tlx 45618.
200 rooms in low-rise blocks and villas arranged around willow-guarded pools and connected by mural-tiled corridors and Chinese bridges. Two swimming pools, sauna, boating, tennis courts, conference centre, Jade City Chinese restaurant. Late Qing Dynasty décor dominates this resort, with stained-glass windows, tasselled lanterns, carved panelling and other assorted chinoiserie. The restaurant is a beauty, with mirrored ceiling vaults, chandeliers, blackwood furniture and waitresses wearing full-length split-skirted cheongsams.

Shijingshan Resort Zhuhai. Tel 22393.
115 rooms in low-rise blocks and bugalows next to the Zhuhai Resort. Two pools, boating, tennis courts, shooting range, hillside garden of sculpted boulders and small pavilions. The Kung Fu Chinese restaurant is rich in late Qing style décor. (For bookings in Macau, tel 553-888, ext 2104.)

Cuiheng Hotel Cuiheng village. Tel 24091.
Opposite the Sun Yat-sen Memorial Park. 242 ranch-style rooms around a pool and garden. Chinese/Western restaurant and disco.

Zhongshan International Hotel 2 Zhongshan Lu, Shiqi. Tel 24788; tlx 44715; fax 24736.
369 rooms in a 20-storey tower in the centre of Shiqi. Pool, sauna, billiards, bowling, revolving restaurant, opulent Chinese restaurant, Western coffee shop. (Book in Hong Kong through China Travel Service, tel 853-3533.)

(facing page) *Kun Iam temple*; (above) *Pou Tai Un temple*; (below) *Kun Iam Temple*

Macao

A weed from Catholic Europe, it took root
Between the yellow mountains and the sea,
And bore these gay stone houses like a fruit,
And grew on China imperceptibly.
Rococo images of Saint and Saviour
Promise her gamblers fortunes when they die;
Churches beside the brothels testify
That faith can pardon natural behaviour.

This city of indulgence need not fear
The major sins by which the heart is killed,
And governments and men are torn to pieces:
Religious clocks will strike; the childish vices
Will safeguard the low virtues of the child;
And nothing serious can happen here.

W H Auden

Through Chinese Eyes

As soon as I entered the wall of Macau, a hundred barbarian soldiers dressed in barbarian military uniform, led by a barbarian headman, greeted me.

At the temple of the God of war I burnt incense and presented the barbarian officials with coloured silks, folding fans, tea and sweetmeats, to the soldiers I gave beer, mutton, wine, flour and 400 pieces of silver.

Then we entered the gate of s. Paulo and going south reached the Niangma Tower, where I burnt incense in front of the image of the Queen of Heaven.

We went the whole length of the Southern Ring Street, getting a general view of the barbarian houses. The barbarians build their houses with one room on top of another sometimes as many as three storeys. The carved doors and green lattices shine from afar like burnished gold. Today the men and women alike are all leaning out of the windows or thronging the side of the streets to see me pass.

Unfortunately barbarian clothes are no match for barbarian houses. The bodies of the men are tightly encased from head to toe by short serge jackets and long close-fitting trousers, so that they look like actors playing the parts of foxes, rabbits and other animals. Their hair is very curly, but they keep it short, not leaving more than an inch or two of curl. They have heavy beards, much of which they shave, leaving one curly turf. Indeed, they do really look like devils, so calling them 'devils' is no empty term of abuse.

They also have devil-slaves who come from the country of the Moors …They are blacker than lacquer, and were this colour from birth.

The barbarian women part their hair in the middle and sometimes even have two partings. Their dresses are cut low exposing their chests, and they wear a double layer of skirt. Marriages are arranged by the young people themselves and people with the same surname are free to marry, which is a barbarous custom.

Lin Tse-hau, Diaries of Lin Tse-hau

Index

A-Ma Temple 39, 45, 53–4
Avenida do Conselheiro Ferreira de Almeida 47, 101

Barra Fort 62, 67–8
Bela Vista Hotel 14, 75, 94–5
Bishop's Palace 75, 85
Bomparto Fort 62

Camões Gardens 45, 103
Camões Museum 45, 90, 91
Carmel Garden 85, 104
Casa Garden 45, 90, 103
Casa Ricci 94
Cathedral 39, 82
Chapel of Our Lady of Guia 66
Chapel of Our Lady of Penha 85
Chapel of Our Lady of Sorrows 83
Chapel of St Francis Xavier 83
Chapel of St James 67
Chapel of St Michael's 106
China Border Gate 72
China City Nightclub 27
Chung Shan (Zhongshan) Golf Course 150
Chung Shan (Zhongshan) Hot Springs 150
Church of Our Lady of Carmel 85, 104
Club Profiteeer 28
Coloane Island 14, 25, 33, 61, 77, 83, 86, 104
Coloane Park 104

Crazy Paris Show 28, 94
Cuiheng 148

Dom Pedro V Theatre 14, 28, 94
Dona Maria Fort 72, 75

Extrada Marginal do Hipodromo 30

Finance Department Tower 102
Fishermen's Bend 33
Flora Gardens 104
Flower City 28
Foshan 148

Government Palace 82, 91
Guangzhou 96, 148
Guia Fort 62, 63, 66–7
Guia Hill 33, 55, 104
Guia Lighthouse 66

Hac Sa Recreational Complex 104
Historical Archives 48
Holy House of Mercy (Santa Casa da Misericordia) 85, 86
Hong Kong Miu (Temple of the Bazaar) 58

Jai Alai Stadium 26

Ka Ho Leper Colony 83
Kam Pek Casino 26
Kun Iam Temple 54

Lappa Island 54
Largo da Sé, see Cathedral
Largo de Sto Agostinho 94
Largo de Senado Square 86
Leal Senado (Loyal Senate) 47, 86–7
Leal Senado Gallery 47
Leal Senado Library 48
Leal Senado Square 78, 85
Lin Fong Miu (Lotus Temple) 55, 58
Lin Kai Miu Temple 59
Lisboa Hotel 26, 102
Lotus Temple, see Lin Fong Miu
Lou Lim Ieoc Garden 43, 47, 103
Loyal Senate, see Leal Senado

Macau Golf and Country Club 31
Macau Grand Prix 33
Macau International Airport 102
Macau Jockey Club 30
Macau Palace Casino 26
Mandarin Oriental Hotel 26
Maritime Museum 45

Military Club 14
Monte Fort 62, 63, 79, 101
Monte Hill 96
Mong-Ha Fort 68, 72–3
Mong-Ha Tourism School 68

National Archives 101
National Library 101
New Protestant Cemetery 106

Old Protestant Cemetery 85, 103, 106

Pearl Land Amusement Park 151
Penha Fort 62
Penha Peninsula 51
Portas do Sol Nightclub 28
Post Office Museum 46
Pou Tai Un Temple 59
Pousada de São Tiago 68
Praia Grande Bay 23, 42, 62, 82, 94, 102

Fortune-teller outside Leal Senado square

Roman Catholic Cemetery of St Michael's 106
Rua do Almirante Sergio 96
Rua de Eduardo Marques 101
Rua das Estalagens 96
Rua das Lorchas 96

Salesian Institute 91
Santa Casa da Misericordia, see Holy House of Mercy
Santa Sancha Palace 91
São Domingos Market 38
São Tiago de Barra, see Barra fort
Shantou 96
Shiqi 145, 148
Skylight Nightclub 28
St Anthony's (Santo Antonio) 85
St Augustine's (Santo Agostinho) 39, 79, 80
St Dominic's (São Domingos) 78, 79
St Francis Fort (São Francisco) 33, 62, 73, 75
St Francis Garden 104
St Joseph's (São José) 82
St Joseph's Seminary 79, 82, 94
St Lawrence's (São Lourenço) 82, 83, 91
St Lazarus (São Lazaro) 51, 85, 101
St Paul's (São Paulo) 51, 59, 75, 77, 78, 96
St Paul's College 75
Stream of Mourning Temple, see Lin Kai Miu

Sun Yat-sen Memorial Home 47, 148
Sun Yat-sen Memorial Hall 144, 149
Sun Yat-sen Museum 148

Tai Soi Mui Temple, see Temple of the Sleeping Buddha
Taipa Diamond 26
Taipa House Museum 46
Taipa Island 25, 33, 59, 75, 85, 95, 102, 104
Taipa Village 14, 46
Tam Kung Temple 61
Temple of the Bazaar, see Hong Kong Miu
Temple of the Sleeping Buddha 59
Tin Hau Temple 59
Tonnochy Nightclub 27

United Chinese Cemetery 107

Vasco da Gama Garden 104

Westin Resort 26
Wharf No 1 45

Xishan Temple 149

Zhongshan 143
Zhuhai Special Economic Zone 145, 149
Zhuhai International Golf Club 150

Tai-chi (above) *Inner Harbour;* (below) *the Parade Ground*